Also by Ronald Hirsch:

Raising a Happy Child: A Practical Guide

Making Your Way in Life as a Buddhist: A Practical Guide

Scratching the Itch: Getting to the Root of our Suffering

The Self in No Self: Buddhist Heresies and Other Lessons of a Buddhist Life

We STILL Hold These Truths: Preserving the Heart of American Democracy for the 21st Century

www.thepracticalbuddhist.com - a Buddhist blog

The end of frustration, fear, and anger.

How to Find Inner Peace

A Handbook For People of
All Faiths and Non-Believers

Ronald L. Hirsch

ThePracticalBuddhist.com Publishing

ISBN 978-1-949756-30-2 (softcover), 978-0-949756-31-9 (eBook).

Published 2019 by ThePracticalBuddhist.com Publishing, Great Barrington, MA 01230, U.S. © 2019 Ronald L. Hirsch. All rights reserved.

No part of this publication may be reproduced, stored in a retrieval system, or transmitted in any form or by any means, electronic, mechanical, recording or otherwise, without the prior written permission of Ronald L. Hirsch.

To all the teachers who, whether through their talks or writings, have guided me in walking the path, encouraged me to persevere, and enabled me ultimately to find the truths from within myself.
To my best friend and life companion, Ken, whose inexhaustible inquisitiveness into life and the mind has brought me into contact with so much wisdom.
And to my friend Bruce, whose unwavering support and love has been a source of comfort to me
for more than 20 years.

TABLE OF CONTENTS

Preface — Peace?.. 1

1. Be Clear What Your Goal Is 11

2. Rediscovering Your True Self... 17
   Our Ego-Mind Is Not Our True Self. 19
   Our True Self Is Our Heart.. 26
   And Our True Nature Is … ?... 33

3. Freeing Your Self... 37
   Form the Intent to Change Your Reaction
      to Things 41
   "Not me!" - Peeling Off the Layers of Our
      Ego-Mind 46
   Discovering the Truth from Within 48
   Change Your Reaction to Things 50
   Healing Your Inner Child.. 62
   Changing the Direction of Your Energy Flow -
      Creating a Forcefield Around You 75
   Just Do It! 79
   Bringing It All Together.. 80

4. Staying Grounded - Being Present................................... 85
   Meditation 88
   Reciting Affirmations... 92
   Reading... 98
   Becoming Part of a Spiritual Community 100
   Applying Spirituality to Daily Life 102

Epilogue-Keep Your Eye on the Prize 107

Appendix I: *Making Your Way in Life as a Buddhist*
Table of Contents 109

Appendix II: Safety Defined 111

Appendix III: 12 Steps on the Buddhist Path 113

About the Author... 119

Preface
Peace?

Peace. What a completely foreign concept this was to me. How can anyone be at peace or serene unless they're a saint? Since I was a young child my life had been filled with inner turmoil, despite an outwardly happy home and relationships. And in looking around at my peers and family, and at the images of the larger culture, I didn't see anyone who was at peace. My parents loved each other, and my friends laughed and relaxed, but that's not peace. Everyone was beset with problems that seriously disturbed them. Even in the idealistic sitcoms of the 50s, whether it was the Beaver, or Ozzie and Harriet, or Lucy ... everyone's lives were filled with conflict and confusion. Yet I knew in my gut that peace and happiness, a life free of suffering, was a rational, reasonable goal. The question was not whether but how?

If you picked up this book and are reading these words, it means that you either realize you're not at peace and want to be, or the sound of the word drew you ... it's something you haven't really thought about, but it resonates and you want it in your life.

First then, what exactly is peace? Peace is the absence of fear, anxiety, hatred, guilt, shame, doubt and confusion ... or better put, it's not the absence of these emotions but not being controlled by them. It's also being free of an intense desire for things you don't have or to be someone other than you are.

FINDING INNER PEACE

When you're under the control of these emotions/desires, you experience suffering; they disturb you, they agitate you, they cause frustration. Just the opposite of a peaceful state of mind. So peace can also be defined as the absence of suffering. And that state allows you to experience happiness. So finding inner peace is definitely a way of being good to yourself.

Since being pulled by these intense emotions/desires are what you've experienced your entire life, it's reasonable that you would ask where and how you can find peace. The first part of the answer is that, believe it or not, peace is within you. You were born with it, it is your natural state, it is your birthright.

But it has been buried beneath an almost impenetrable layer of the detritus of your life experiences. So the second part of finding peace is a process of reconnecting with that part of you that's been lost. That is is the subject of this book ... the process.

Peace was taken away from you almost from the moment of your birth and by most of the life experiences you've had since.

Birth, being thrust out of the womb, has to be a scary experience. When an animal is born, it is typically licked all over by the mother and is always next to the mother's warmth until weaned. But when a baby is born, it is slapped on the behind, washed by a stranger, rolled up in a blanket and given to its mother to be held and fed before being put in a basinet by itself. Not a nurturing environment,

When a child is born, he has four basic needs: food, freedom from pain, warmth/nurturing, and physical security. These are the four irreducible needs of all human beings.[1] In particular, a baby's need for nurturing, for unconditional love, is almost without limit. So from the

---

[1] Ronald Hirsch, *The Self in No Self*, ThePracticalBuddhist.com Publishing, 2012, pp. 108-114

moment of its birth, a baby finds that its needs are not met, and the first seeds of insecurity are sown.

This pattern continues during the child's formative first years. It's not that parents don't love their new child and shower it with attention; it's that the needs of the baby and toddler go beyond what most parents are able to give. Whether it's how they were raised, the demands of work or home, or having their own problems to deal with ... it's just the way it is.

As the baby becomes a young child, proceeds through adolescence, and attains adulthood, the seeds of insecurity planted at birth and during his formative years grow to become a huge tumor inside each of us. Why?

The tumor grows because it's fed by much of what we experience in life ... at home, in school, at work, and in the media. We don't feel respected or loved. We are either told or learn that we are clearly lacking in some way. If we want to be loved or admired, we learn that we must change something in ourselves or acquire something. Or if we are praised, we nevertheless understand how easy it is to fall from grace and so are fearful. In fact, those who become famous or successful, although they are often thought of as having huge egos and are imperious, typically have even greater insecurities than the average person because their success is a coping mechanism and they have more to lose.

Because this insecurity runs so deep and is so threatening to us, our mind ... what I will refer to in this book as the ego-mind ... develops a host of strategies to "protect" us. If it feels we have been treated badly by others, for example, it will throw up a wall of anger or disdain which gives us a feeling of self-righteousness that obscures the hurt. If it feels we need to do more to achieve success or happiness, it creates cravings and attachments that drive us to get what we need at all costs.

But these strategies do not in fact protect us; instead, they cause us suffering. Yet we take comfort in these familiar emotions/desires because we believe they do protect us or provide us with a path to achieving happiness.

And so every person, each and every one of us, ends up a prisoner of their ego-mind ... of the feelings and perceptions, emotions, judgments, cravings, and attachments that are the mind's reaction to our life experiences. Our every action and thought is controlled by our feelings and perceptions. The habit-energy is ingrained.

Why do I call the ego-mind a prison? Because it has over the years erected a high, almost impenetrable, wall. It may have been built to protect us, and we may feel comforted by the wall, a sense of security, but it also contains us, separates us, prevents us from experiencing ourselves and the world around us directly, free of our feelings and perceptions. Inside this wall we don't grow stronger; we become a victim of our emotions, we suffer, we atrophy.

And because our intense desires, while not a wall, are without question chains from which no amount of sheer willpower can free us. Even if we have the presence of mind to try and stop these forces, it is of no avail.

In this way we have ended up with a world full of insecure people grasping at things outside themselves for security and walling off anything which offends or threatens. We each compensate for it, mask it, in many ways, but the insecurity is still there.

What are the consequences? In a word, human relations are fraught with conflict ... first and foremost our relationship with ourselves. We are full of self-doubt and anxiety. We do not love ourselves or have compassion for ourselves. How sad!

This in turn creates conflict with the world around us. All the fighting, abuse, hatred, and discrimination ... whether within the family, within society, or between nations ... all are at their core a function of man's insecurity.

PREFACE

And so we all suffer. This is the universal state of man.[2] The evidence is all around you ... you are not alone in not experiencing peace. We live in a world of turmoil ... unrest, dysfunction, and conflict everywhere. And as a direct result of that turmoil, billions of innocent people are damaged, most psychologically but many economically and physically as well.

In the annals of human history, this is not only nothing new, this is the norm. The question that naturally must be asked is, "Why?"

Most would say that it is human nature to be in conflict. It is human nature for some to aggressively seek what they want and others to either respond aggressively to protect themselves or to submit to greater power. We each have our needs and they are in conflict with others'. Certainly this describes the world we experience and so understandably seems for most to be the natural order. We truly cannot imagine things being any different. It is our learned experience, the way we have been acculturated to life.

The reader may well support that view, adding that much of what I said in the preceding paragraph also describes very closely the activity we see in nature in the fight for dominance within a group. And this is true. But as with other basic evolutionary forces such as fear, man's ego-mind has taken these natural forces and morphed them exponentially into the dysfunction and suffering we see in "modern" man.

Instead, I and many far more learned and wise men over the centuries would say that this is not evidence of human nature. This is rather the result of human development. Thus change is possible. Man does have a choice.

---

[2] It therefore also makes us ripe fodder for the "religion'" of consumerism, of materialism, which both fosters and feeds off our insecurity.

From the very beginning, man was cast into a challenging world over which he had no control. But we know from studying indigenous people, especially those of Australia and Africa, that for millennia mankind lived a communal life where all were cared for and valued. They were not insecure. And they felt one with nature.[3] Yes, there were outside forces, other tribes, that could threaten, but that did not disturb their feeling of inner security.

At some point in its development though, mankind ceased the communal life, lost that enveloping sense of security, and lost the sense of oneness with nature. The fear that resulted from this new insecurity became a basic component of early non-animist religions. Including a fear of death which did not exist previously.[4]

Whereas previously one's sense of security lay in knowing one was part of the eternal cycle of nature, these new religions taught that salvation/protection lay in prayer to a higher power.[5] And some men learned to use others' insecurity and weakness to gain power for themselves and thereby ward off their own insecurity

Thus the basic dynamic of man's insecurity - his looking to something outside himself for security, and man's abusing his fellow man for his own benefit - came into being. And with each succeeding generation that dynamic was strengthened and human neuroses further entrenched as insecure parents raised insecure children who grew up to become insecure parents who ...

Today, this is still the dynamic. It is a very powerful, deeply-rooted force. Some would say that it is stronger than

---

[3] The Australian Museum, "Family," https://australianmuseum.net.au/indigenous-australia-family;
James Suzman, *Affluence Without Abundance: The Disappearing World of the Bushmen*, Bloomsbury USA, 2017

[4] Kristoffer Hughes, *The Journey Into Spirit: A Pagan's Perspective on Death*, Llewellyn Publications, 2014

[5] In animist religions, people would also pray for good crops or health, but it was out of respect, not insecurity or fear.

PREFACE

ever. But because it is a dynamic that has been impressed upon man, because it is not his natural state, you can with faith and discipline free yourself from its control.

"Where is the proof," the reader may well ask, "that contrary to all this circumstantial and damning evidence inner peace is our natural state?" The "proof," beyond what we know of aboriginal/indigenous man, is that the mystical traditions of all three Abrahamic faiths ... Judaism, Christianity, and Islam ... as well as Buddhism and Hinduism contain the same teaching: that the true nature of man is peace and goodness. And this is not just religious thinking; the same teaching can be found in the classic Greek philosophies that speak to how we should live life ... Epicureanism, Stoicism, and Skepticism.

For most readers the statement I just made will be a shock.[6] This is not what you've heard in your church, synagogue, or mosque. For Catholics and followers of many Christian denominations, you've actually been taught just the opposite - the doctrine of original sin ... that we are all born sinners; hardly men of peace and goodness.

The reason why you've not heard this teaching is that there's a big difference between the teaching of the religious establishments and their mystical traditions. Let me very briefly present proof that the common teaching of these traditions is that the God-essence and thus peace is our true

---

[6] For those of you who are Buddhists, the teachings I present in these first pages will not be new to you. Indeed much of what I say in the book may not be new to you. But if you've picked up this book, that indicates you are struggling on the path; your ego-mind still has a firm grip on you and so you have not made much progress and are suffering. The approach I present is an amalgam of what I've learned from various teachers as well as my own experience walking the path and helping others. I hope this approach to the Buddha dharma will enable you to finally find peace, to free yourself from the intervention of your ego-mind.

self, not our ego.[7] They further teach, however, that our true nature is unknown to us; it has been concealed from us. And so it is for us to rediscover it, to uncover it, and allow it to embrace us and transform us.

- Christian Gnosticism teaches that the human true self is a fragment of the divine essence, the "divine spark." But we are "ignorant of our true origins and our essential nature" because forces cause us to remain attached to earthly things that keep us enslaved. It is this ignorance which brings about sin; man is not inherently sinful. Salvation from that ignorance is stimulated by the teachings of others, such as those of Christ, but man must ultimately find his own truth.[8]
- According to Jewish Kabbalah, "every soul is pure in essence and the only salvation is to become enlightened (i.e. to remember the truth of who and what we really are). ... Salvation is the process of clearing out whatever obstructs our manifestation of the concealed divine image. ... Kabbalah leads to the conclusion that ultimately we must rely on ourselves - for we alone have the power to save ourselves." It is to our heart we must look for guidance, not our ego-mind.[9]

---

[7] The reader may raise an eyebrow here. Christ was certainly a man of peace, but many of us were taught that the God of the Old Testament was a wrathful God; hardly a God of peace. This "fact," however, is the product of the men who wrote the Bible; fear was a way of controlling man.

[8] The Gnosis Archive, http://gnosis.org/gnintro.htm

[9] "What does the soul mean in Kabbalah?"
http://www.hebrew4christians.com/Articles/kabbalah/The_Soul/the_soul.html;
"What Is a Soul?"
http://www.chabad.org/library/article_cdo/aid/3194/jewish/What-is-a-Soul.htm

PREFACE

- Islamic Sufism is again about the journey of self-realization. Sufi means "unfoldment of the spirit towards its original condition." That original self is the Divine presence in man's heart. Our heart is love, faith, trust, compassion, wisdom, and peace. Insecurity is a product of the mind. When one truly knows oneself, one knows God. "He has to find God within himself, but He can only be found in a heart that has been purified by the fire of love [of God]."[10]

We cannot change the world around us. It is what it is. And we cannot change our past. But as the mystical traditions and the Buddha teach, and as the Serenity Prayer says,[11] we can change how we relate to ourselves and the world around us and thus change how we experience life; we can change our life experience from suffering to peace.

The purpose of this book is to empower you, to give you the tools you will need to free yourself from the prison of your ego-mind, to free yourself from the identity you thought was you and instead discover your true self and change how you experience yourself and the world around you. To find your inner peace.

Ever since my belated exposure to the teachings of the Buddha (I was 49), I have had deep faith in those teachings. They were credible; they made sense of what never had made sense to me.

The knowledge of this commonality across often (historically) antagonistic religious and philosophical lines

---

[10] Hazrat Inayat Khan, *Personality: The Art of Being and Becoming*, Omega Press, 1982;
Sufi Principles & Practices,
http://www.sufisaints.net/index.php?option=com_content&view=article&id=49&Itemid=55;
Practices of Sufism,
http://www.beautyislam.org/practices_of_sufism.html

[11] A widely used prayer written by the famous American theologian Reinhold Niebuhr. See Chapter 4.

has strengthened my already deep faith in this truth about the nature of man. If one does need proof that the natural state of man is his God essence/Buddha nature, that he is a man of peace and happiness, to me the universality of this teaching provides such proof.

I should note at the outset that I am approaching this question of man's nature, and indeed the entire book, from the perspective of a Buddhist. But regardless whether you are a Christian, Jew, or Muslim, or practice no religion, the message of this book, as I have noted, is supported by the mystical teaching of your religion as well as secular philosophy. It's our culture that is in conflict.

Now it is time to begin the process of finding, of rediscovering, the peace and happiness that lies within *you*, within your heart. As you work through the process ... and it is without any question work, for you are changing the paradigms that have governed your life; it will require discipline and perseverance ... always keep foremost in your mind why you are doing this: you want to bring peace and happiness into your life. You want peace to be the norm, not suffering.

And never forget that you do have a choice. You don't have to remain a prisoner of your ego-mind and continue to suffer. You can summon the courage to free yourself, to open the door and step into the world of your true self ... a space filled with light, love, faith, trust, compassion, gratefulness, joy, and peace that you have not known since you were a smiling toddler.

The other morning when I meditated, I happened to focus on a clear spot in the oak flooring that was surrounded by the swirling grains of the wood. As I sat, I saw it as the eye of a hurricane. Which in turn I realized was what my heart, my true Buddha nature is. It is the place of peace and calm in the midst of the swirling emotions of my ego-mind and the events of the world around me. That is the space I want to help you find within yourself.

I wish you all a good journey.

Chapter 1:
Be Clear What Your Goal Is

In the preface, we established that since you're reading this book, you are at least entertaining the goal of making peace and happiness the norm of your life, not suffering. This may sound like a no-brainer, a "duh!" statement. But believe me, it's not.

Most of the people in your immediate circle suffer, as do most of the people in the nation and the world. Whether rich or poor, successful or not, regardless of the color of their skin, their faith, their gender, their sexual orientation ... all people suffer.

You suffer too. But you, unlike most people in the world, are fortunately both aware that you do in fact suffer ... all is not well ... and are able to at least entertain the idea that your life could be different. That peace may be an option for you.

That thought is huge. It opens the door, at least a crack, to transformations that will change your life for the better.

The other reason why your tentative embrace of this concept is not a no-brainer is that the transformation from suffering to experiencing peace and happiness does not come easy. It requires a lot of work, discipline, and perseverance.

This is why it is so important to be clear what your goal is. Only with that clarity will you be able to withstand the pressures coming both from your ego-mind and from the environment that surrounds you ... family, friends, work, media, culture ... and so stay your course to find inner peace.

In the preface, I said the process is difficult because it

entails changing the paradigms that have governed your life, the way you relate to yourself and the world around you. What exactly does that mean?

If I were to ask most people what would make them happy, they would probably answer with some combination of people/relationships that would come into their life, successes/money they would have, or things they would acquire. All things that give a sense of security. And what most people crave is security, safety. They would not answer, "being at peace."

Likewise, if I were to ask most people for their reaction to their life experiences and those around them, they would certainly answer with many positive thoughts, but at the same time they would also certainly express feelings of anger, resentment, fear, anxiety, negativity. They would not answer, "compassion."

There you have it ... the basic conundrum facing those wanting to bring peace into their lives, to end their suffering. Because of their life experiences and the culture we live in, people want what they want, they feel what they feel. *And* they are quite adamant about the reasonableness of their desires and the righteousness of their feelings. Do you recognize yourself in this?

But their attachment to these feelings and perceptions is the very thing that makes a life of peace and happiness impossible because that attachment brings nothing but frustration and suffering. The same is true for security; it was only after I stopped searching for security that I finally felt secure. You can't have your cake and eat it too. Note that it is the attachment, the obsession, that is the problem, not the feeling and perception itself.

These two questions expose the rift between our culture and one's happiness and security. In our culture, happiness/security is primarily defined by advertising and media images as having/acquiring the things and being the kind of person that make for the "good" life. The more money one has and therefore the greater ability to acquire

BE CLEAR WHAT YOUR GOAL IS

things, or the more one is like the handsome, successful, confident people portrayed, the happier one will be. And so by implication, to be poor, to not have the ability to acquire the accoutrements of the good life, to be unattractive or a "failure," is to be unhappy and insecure.

Yet as any psychologist will attest, neither happiness nor inner security derives from the accumulation of material things, attaining success, or physical beauty. It certainly results in a level of material comfort and self-satisfaction, and provides a sense/illusion of security, but that does not equate with happiness or inner peace and security.

Rather, our cultural obsession or addiction with acquiring things and being more than we are leads to high levels of dissatisfaction, frustration, and depression. When someone always wants what one doesn't have, or more of what one does have, there may be momentary periods where acquiring something or reaching a certain status brings a sense of satisfaction. But that passes rather quickly as the ego-mind focuses on the next thing one needs to acquire or be to fulfill its craving, and thus comes the inevitable frustration.

Related to the myth that having many things or being more than we are brings happiness is the obsession among many people with achieving not just wealth but the status and power that comes with wealth. Being looked up to by others, being envied, even feared, and having power over others is supposed to bring increased security and thus happiness. But again, any psychologist will tell you this is also a myth.

So if the shibboleths of happiness in our culture are in fact not good predictors of happiness, what is?

There is a Buddhist saying, "Happiness comes from within." That means that it does not spring from nor is dependent on anything external to oneself. On the contrary, such dependence only causes frustration and unhappiness.

To find that happiness, to be able to be one with your heart, you must free yourself from the control of the feelings and perceptions that flow from your ego-mind. Only then can you reconnect with your true self and experience peace and happiness. It is, as I said before, about freeing yourself from the prison of your mind.

To that end, I noted in the preface that it was important to keep foremost in your mind why you have started this process: you want to bring peace and happiness into your life; you want that to be the norm, not suffering. This point cannot be overstated.

But this intent must be more than lip service. To walk the path you are undertaking, you will need to be able to withstand the insistent screams of your ego-mind: "But I want ...!" or "I don't want to accept the way things are!" or "I have every right to be angry! I have to stand up for myself!" To withstand that inner pressure, to act in what is truly your best interest, you must be very clear on what's most important to you.

To be absolutely clear, it bears repeating that this does not mean that you live a static life or that you let life roll over you; that you have to give up desires, stop trying to improve your life, or stop feeling what you feel or having your opinions. Walking the path does not mean getting rid of your feelings and perceptions.

It *does* mean freeing yourself from the control of your feelings and perceptions, which means changing how you approach life experiences. Basically, changing from acting out of emotion to acting from a place of equanimity and always being true to yourself.

So, now I'm going to ask you the question: What is it that you value most? What is most important to you?

It is likely that, despite the fact you are reading this book because you want to bring peace and happiness into your life, your initial answer will be something else. If so, ask why that is important. Keep going deeper.

What you will find is that in the end it all comes down to peace and happiness. Whether you say you want material security, money, love ... whatever ... we want these things

BE CLEAR WHAT YOUR GOAL IS

because we believe, or have been taught, they will bring us peace and happiness.

Your answer to this question will have a very practical application as you continue on the path to find inner peace. That is why clarity on this question is so important.

Briefly stated, you will use your desire for peace and happiness as a touchstone against which to test what you are thinking or doing. If it causes you suffering, then you will reject that thought or action either because it is harmful in and of itself, or because although it is good for you, you are approaching it in a way that causes you suffering. I know this sounds obtuse, so here are some examples.

If you desire to do anything with the intent of harming someone else, that is an action that in and of itself is spiritually harmful to you and you should reject it.

But let's say you have a desire to make friends, find a lover, or have good health; these are all Right desires which can bring you peace and happiness.[12] However, if you approach these things with an obsession, with a fear of what will result if you are not successful, then they become cravings and you will experience frustration and suffering. Instead you will need to find a way to approach these desires with equanimity so that you experience peace and happiness regardless what happens.

Or if you feel angry and resentful at what someone has done to you. The problem is not that you feel someone has acted improperly towards you; it's that your emotions have taken control, turning hurt into anger, and so you suffer. The answer is not to just roll over, but to take action on your grievance from a place of equanimity. More on testing and rejecting your guidance and how to act and react with equanimity in all situations in Chapter 3.

Such is the power of the ego-mind that being clear on

---

[12] The Buddha defines eight Right activities that lead to peace. One of these is Right effort, which is in part the desire to develop wholesome states.

what's most important to you is just the first step. In order to follow through and reject the guidance of your ego-mind with any consistency, to have the strength and the will to withstand its power, you will need to first rediscover your true self (Chapter 2) and then go through a process of freeing yourself from the control of your ego-mind (Chapter 3).

Chapter 2:
Rediscovering Your True Self

Because we so strongly identify with our ego-mind, in order to rediscover our true self, we must first understand and accept that we are not who we thought we were. Depending on your self-perception, this may be viewed by you as a mixed thing ... good news/bad news. But in fact, viewed from the perspective of achieving peace and happiness in your life, it's all good news.

For example, if you view yourself as a catalog of negative labels ... bad, stupid, failure, ugly, whatever ... your true self is none of those labels. You are who you are, free of any of the pejorative labels that your family, peers, or culture have saddled you with. Moreover, you actually have special qualities which have likely been overlooked by everyone, including yourself; everyone has something special about them.

On the other hand, if you view yourself as someone special, a paragon in whatever way, your true self again is none of those things. You are just who you are. You have your talents or qualities, but that doesn't make you more special than the next person. *Every person is special.* You're just fortunate that you've had the opportunity to uncover your specialness; most haven't. We are all in the same boat. No one is more deserving than the next.

This bears repeating. What I am saying does not gainsay whatever true talents you have or whatever blemishes you may have. This process does not take away your individuality. What I am saying is that the labels we have applied to ourselves set up expectations, whether positive or negative, that cause us endless suffering.

If we apply negative labels to ourselves, this last statement has an immediate evident truth. But even if you think of yourself as special, in the sense of being better than others, while this may seem like a great ego-boost, in fact it sets you up for the ongoing fear of losing that specialness or being eclipsed by someone else. It also sets you up for frustration when you aren't treated in the way in which you think you deserve to be treated. This is why so many of the rich and famous are imperious and otherwise insufferable. There is rarely any grace about them.

So, let us first turn to discovering who you are not.

REDISCOVERING YOUR TRUE SELF

1. Our Ego-Mind Is Not Our True Self.

It is the teaching of all the spiritual/mystical traditions that our ego-mind is not our true self. Our ego-mind is an accretion of all our life experiences ... the labels we are taught to apply to ourselves and others, the ways in which we have been wounded, and all our ways of reacting to those experiences.[13] None of these labels or reactions are inherent in us; they are a product of the mind.

But so powerful is the ego-mind, so completely do we identify with it, that we view ourselves and the world around us through its perspective. That is our sole reality. Only by rediscovering our true self will we experience a true, unbiased reality and thus find peace and happiness.

My favorite way to clarify the difference between things as they are and the way we perceive them through our mind is our relationship with the weather. The weather is what it is. It is factual. The temperature is so many degrees. It rains or is sunny. Yet depending on where we grew up and our life experiences, we react to these circumstances in very different ways.

For people who grew up in the South, a hot, humid day is wonderful. For someone who grew up in the far north, such a day is unbearable. The reverse is true when the temperature drops down to 0 degrees. Likewise there are many people who find the endless grey, rainy winter days of the Northwest depressing, while many who were born there find them either nourishing or a non-issue.

The point is that the weather is the weather; it is factual. The labels we apply, however, are entirely subjective and a product of our life experiences. And yet those labels often have an enormous influence on our sense of well-being.

---

[13] The ego-mind is that part of your mind that forms value judgments, emotions, perspectives. It is distinct from that part of your mind that is purely functional ... how to add 2 + 2, how to get from point A to point B.

They have the power to make us feel miserable and unwell or just fine ... all under the same objective circumstances. If you say the weather is unbearable, it will indeed feel unbearable.

And so it goes with our relationship with ourselves and the world around us. There are two ways in which our life experiences form our ego-mind, our self-perception. The first is how we react to people doing or saying things that directly impact us. The second are the messages we receive from the broader culture.

The deepest and most far-reaching aspect of our ego-mind that is a function of our life-experience is the insecurity that virtually all human beings develop. As I explained in the preface, this is a learned experience; it is not our natural state. From the moment of our birth through our early development years, because babies and young children do not receive the nurturing that they need from their parents, we all develop a deep insecurity that remains with us throughout our lives.

During our later childhood, adolescence and adulthood, anything we experience that can be viewed through that lens of insecurity will be viewed that way. It will be taken as verification that we are not loved, we are not wanted, we are not valued or respected.

We always, perversely, view things through our wounded selves, what is often called our wounded inner child, and thus suffer emotionally, psychologically. Not only do we suffer, but we make others suffer because our insecurity often causes us to act towards them aggressively or coldly.

Other aspects of our self-image are to a large extent formed by the way other people see us (or how we think they see us). During childhood and adolescence, our immediate family and circle of peers have an enormous power over our self-image. For example, if we are called "stupid" repeatedly, or if we are called "bad" repeatedly, we come to view ourselves as stupid or bad, which often becomes a self-fulfilling prophesy. Likewise if friends and family fawn over us, we will view ourselves as special and worthy of that attention. In both cases, the underlying reality, our truth, is overwhelmed and rendered irrelevant. We may at times question these labels, question their truth, but for the most part they stick.

Our immediate environment also influences how we view others, the world around us. As the song from *South Pacific* says, "You've got to be taught before you are six, or seven, or eight to hate all the people your relatives hate, you've got to be carefully taught." And these judgments often stay with us throughout our lives, sometimes playing a dominant role, sometimes more subsurface.

The broader culture impacts us through the images projected by the media, whether through marketing or otherwise, of what we need to do to be happy, to be wanted, to be loved. The insecurity we develop in childhood makes us fodder for these messages. Whether it's the urging to acquire things, to dress a certain way, to look attractive, and on and on ... we absorb the marketing directed at us and its message that these things/attributes are the key to happiness and success.

And so, we either do what we can to follow that advice and become obsessed with attaining the desired qualities, or if that's either beyond our financial means or our physicality we become depressed or angry and often develop substance addictions to cope with these feelings. We compare ourselves to these marketing images and label ourselves, negatively or positively, in response. These labels form our self-image and both types are harmful to us.

It's relatively easy for most people to understand and accept that they are the way they are in large part because of their life experiences. They may not be happy about it, and blame others, but it conforms with their observed reality.

But how can one go on to say that all these things that flow from our ego-mind are not me? The first thing to understand, and this is not double talk, is that in one sense these emotions and perceptions are you ... they definitely are part of your ego-mind. They will thus always be a part of you because it is not a goal of spiritual practice to get rid of or sanitize your ego-mind. Instead the goal is to rediscover your true self and free yourself from the control of your ego-mind.

As to how one can say that the feelings and perceptions that flow from the ego-mind are not the real you, the answer is very straight forward. The Buddha once asked his disciples whether a thought or feeling caused them suffering. If it did, he said, "this is not you, this is not yours, this is not your self, for your self would not cause you suffering."

This is a basic truth: *No one's true self would cause them suffering*. So the next step in understanding that your ego-mind is not your true self is to be aware and acknowledge the fact that the feelings and perceptions that flow from your ego-mind cause you suffering.

Think about it. If you apply negative labels to yourself, it won't be hard for you to be aware and accept that your feelings and perceptions cause you suffering. Calling ourselves, for example, ugly or stupid or fat is obviously harmful. It is degrading. (Whereas acknowledging that we are plain or not intelligent or weigh a certain amount is not degrading. If we can separate the facts from the labels that will be clear.) These labels keep us from maximizing our potential because they hold us back; we feel we are not worthy, we will not be accepted.

Likewise, when we apply such negative labels to those around us, whether family or strangers, it creates a barrier and separates us from them. Which in a different way also keeps us from maximizing our potential, our relationship with the world around us.

But if you generally apply positive labels to yourself, then you may have to go through some serious introspection to see clearly that your feelings and perceptions about yourself and the world around you cause you suffering.

Positive labels are harmful because they are a trap. We believe the marketing and society's message that if we have money, if we have a certain lifestyle, if we are physically attractive, etc., that we will be happy. But in reality that does not follow. Hardly.

Most people are unhappy despite attaining these things or having these attributes. As I explained briefly above, this can happen in several ways. If you feel you are special in one or many ways, that typically sets up expectations that you deserve certain experiences in life, that you deserve to be respected, acknowledged, etc. And so each time you're not, it's a cause of frustration and suffering. So, for example, I recently read that when Patti LuPone did not get the film part of Evita, she was so depressed that it took a year of therapy for her to recover. She thought it was her due, and when she didn't get it it almost destroyed her.

Second, no matter how good you have it, how successful you are, you will always want more. It's the nature of the beast. You also fear losing what you have, whether through your own action ... for example aging ... or being eclipsed by someone else. This is strictly speaking as much a result of your insecurity as your opinion of yourself creating the expectation that you deserve more and more, but the two go hand in hand. So again, for example, Joan Rivers was a very successful comedian, even as she got older. Frequent club dates all over the country. But in a documentary, she shows the interviewer her schedule; there were a few empty days that month. She said that any empty dates (that weren't travel days) killed her. She felt a failure!!

Before moving on with the book, I ask that you very carefully examine all aspects of your self-image ... your ego-mind's take on the reality of you. Be aware of all the labels you apply to yourself, both positive and negative, and become aware of how they cause you suffering.

The point, again, is not to dispute or disown the physical or mental facts of your being, or the talents you have or don't have. The point is to see how the labels we apply to ourselves, that the ego-mind applies to ourselves, usually by comparing ourselves with others, cause us to obsess about these things and cause us suffering.

Also examine your feelings and perceptions ... your emotions, judgments, cravings, and attachments ... towards the world around you, both immediate and far. Become aware of how these too cause you suffering.

As you undertake this exercise, it's very important to be aware of the difference between pain and hurt on the one hand and suffering on the other. Pain and hurt is real; it happens. Suffering is a product of the mind; it is in the psyche. For example, when you are sick or have an accident, the pain is real. But when you become gripped with fear about what you are experiencing or what the future may hold, that is the mind asserting itself with it's endless "what if's;" its obsessive worry about the future. It's the fear that ties you up in knots and debilitates you, not the illness or accident.

This exercise is important not just to understand that your ego-mind is not your true self. Your goal is to bring more peace and happiness into your life. That means first understanding why it is that you don't have peace and happiness now; why you suffer.

If you continue to think you suffer because of the way you're treated or what life has thrown your way or the way the world around you operates, then there is no way to end your suffering because you can't change the world or even those close to you; you can't change the facts of life. You will suffer because you feel your peace and happiness is dependent on external forces.

Only when you come to realize and acknowledge that you suffer solely because of your feelings and perceptions ... the way your ego-mind relates to yourself and reacts to your life experience and the world around you ... will you find the door to freeing yourself from that suffering, to finding inner peace. Because you *do* have the power to control how you relate to yourself and the world around you. That is the basis of the serenity prayer, "Lord, grant me the serenity to accept the things I cannot change, and the courage to change the things I can."

But acknowledging that how you've been treated by life is not the cause of your suffering, rather it's how your ego-mind has reacted to those events, does not come easily. You, which is to say your ego-mind, will revolt at this thought; we are used to blaming the world and take odd comfort in that. But please note that this is not a "blame game;" you are not instead now blaming your ego; you have compassion for it. It's just understanding the truth, reality.

And so you need to carefully examine the things that push your buttons. Try and discern the difference between the hurt or pain caused by the experience and the turmoil/suffering caused by your anger or hatred or fear, for example, which was your reaction to the experience.

Now that you've gone through the process of learning that your ego-mind, your feelings and perceptions, are not your true self and even are the cause of your suffering, how do you learn or rediscover who you truly are?

2. Our True Self Is Our Heart.

"Who am I?" This is not only a very legitimate question, it is central to the spiritual process of freeing ourselves from suffering, of finding peace.

Until you know without doubt that your true self is your heart, your God-essence ... not just intellectually but identify with it ... you will not know that you have everything you need inside yourself to be at peace and happy; you will not have faith that regardless what is going on around you or happening to you that all will be well because you will always return home to your heart and be at peace and happy. And so you will not be able to withstand the powerful pull of your ego-mind.

Understanding that your true self is not your ego-mind is a necessary step and helpful, in and of itself. But it is not sufficient to free you from suffering and find peace and happiness. For that, it needs to be replaced by a positive concept ... you must know that your true self is your heart, your God-essence.

But for most of us humans, such language is all a bit too abstract. For years, this question of who I am was a puzzlement for me. I believed the teaching that my true self was my true Buddha nature, my unborn Buddha mind. But what was that? I had no experience of that (or so I thought). I couldn't wrap my head around the concept. And so while I mouthed the truths as a mantra, it did nothing to move my practice forward.

Then one day when I was meditating, I saw a photo of me as a smiling toddler in my mind's eye. Happy, open, unwounded, smiling for no reason at all other than just being. I knew at that moment that was my true Buddha nature, and I wept, tears rolling down my cheeks.

I was able to have that experience because a few days earlier my mother had sent me my baby book together with photos of myself from that period of my life. Obviously those photos made a deep impression on me.

REDISCOVERING YOUR TRUE SELF

We forget there was a time when we were not engulfed by suffering, when we had not yet felt wounded by life, when the joyfulness in our heart shone and we were a light unto ourselves and others. Those photos brought that awareness back to me with a real force.

I strongly encourage you to find a photo of yourself as a smiling toddler to connect with. If one is not available, conjure up such an image in your mind's eye.

Even though the wounding process starts shortly after birth for most of us, we are as toddlers remarkably resilient. Just think of all the wide-eyed, smiling toddlers you've seen. These are not children who have not had negative experiences in their short life, yet their spirit is still flowing from their heart; they have not lost faith that they will be nurtured and loved.

That happens a little later (around age 3) when the ego-mind develops and children begin storing feelings based on their experiences. At that point, the feelings "unloved" and "neglected," among many others, enter the psyche.

For those of you who think that regardless what you may have been as a toddler, that spirit is irretrievably lost, that pure spirit is not within you any more, reflect on this. Have you never had a moment when you experienced an internal discussion between what we often refer to as the "good" me and the "bad" me over what to do?

Where do you think these voices come from? The angry, distrustful, hurt voice comes from the ego-mind. The voice which is full of compassion comes from your heart. That is the voice of your God-essence/your true Buddha nature.

This experience, which we all have had, often with some regularity, is proof that our true self, our spirit, is not irretrievably lost. It is just usually drowned out, overpowered, by the volume and force of our ego-mind.

Before I move on, look at this terminology; another example of how we label ourselves. We call part of us "bad" because it's doing something we've been told is bad or just not the thing to do. But no part of us is bad. We are what we are, without any value judgments. We may do hurtful or bad things, but we are not bad. The same goes for being "good." More on not labeling ourselves, embracing all aspects of our being in Chapter 3.

So now that you understand you do have this inviolate source of purity within you, how do you get a better feel for your heart? How do you connect with, tune yourself to your heart?

The first step is to start learning to love yourself, unconditionally. By this I don't mean thinking that you're great, or smart, or any other superlative. Or that you are free to do whatever you want regardless who is harmed or what the impact.

I mean spiritually loving yourself for being the person you are, just as you are, warts and all. This unconditional love does not mean, as I explained earlier, that you are absolved of responsibility for your actions. But you do not turn that responsibility into feelings that you are a guilty or a shameful, bad person.[14]

One way of doing this is to practice *tonglen* on yourself. This is described helpfully in Sogyal Rinpoche's *Tibetan Book of Living and Dying*. Tonglen is the Tibetan practice of receiving and giving ... receiving the suffering and pain of others and giving them your happiness, well-being, and peace of mind. Rinpoche recommends starting this practice by first doing it for yourself, for before one can have compassion for others, one has to have compassion for oneself.

The first step is to *"unseal the spring of loving kindness."* To do that he suggests going back in your mind and recreate, visualize, a love that someone gave you that really moved you. My mind wandered through several possibilities both in my adult life and childhood, when suddenly I

---

[14] For more on the difference between healthy shame and toxic shame see my post, "Shame," at www.thepracticalbuddhist.com

remembered an instance with my father that was repeated often when I was small. When he would come home from a long day's work, he would come to me in my bed and play with my toes ... "This little piggy went to market, this little piggy stayed home, this little piggy worked in the garden, and this little piggy ran all the way home!" ... making me laugh and very happy.

When I remembered that episode, which had long since been forgotten, I cried because of the love that I was feeling from my father and almost simultaneously a big smile formed on my face.[15] Rinpoche says that, *"You will remember then that even though you may not always feel that you have been loved enough, you were loved genuinely once. Knowing that now will make you feel again that you are, as that person made you feel then, worthy of love and really lovable."* And so it did.

Under his further instruction, I let my heart open and the love that flowed from it was extended to my father, to my family and friends, and others. I visualized holding my father as he was dying (I was not there in fact) and saying to him, "You can let go now for I know that you love me and I love you ... I will be ok." I was now ready to practice tonglen on myself.

Rinpoche suggests, for the purpose of this exercise, dividing yourself into two aspects ... one is the aspect of you that is whole, compassionate, etc. - your smiling toddler; the other is the aspect of you that has been hurt, that feels misunderstood, bitter or angry, *"who might have been unjustly treated or abused as a child, or has suffered in relationships or been wronged by society,"* - your wounded inner child. As you breathe in, your smiling toddler opens its heart completely and receives all of your wounded inner child's pain and suffering. As you breathe out, the first aspect gives the other all its healing love, warmth, trust, and happiness. In

---

[15] For you to understand the force of this memory, I have to share with you that for most of my life, say past age 5 or 6, I felt unloved by my father.

response, the other aspect opens its heart to this love and all suffering melts away in this embrace.

What could be more appropriate for me given my history, I thought! And so, I practiced tonglen on myself with beneficial results. Indeed, as the weeks and months passed after this experience, I practiced both the visualization of my father's love as well as tonglen on myself on a regular basis. Each time I did, I felt that smile ... the smile of happiness and love ... form naturally and for many weeks tears would roll down my cheeks. Clearly, this was a very cathartic experience for me.

Once you have done this exercise, you will be ready to tune your heart, to fully connect with your heart. I learned how to do this from a Sufi book, *Personality - The Art of Being and Becoming*, by Hazrat Khan.

He teaches that for the heart to be tuned to the right pitch, "it must have a certain awakening, a certain amount of life in it, that can only be brought about by sympathy." And what is inner sympathy? It is a combination of kindness, mercy, goodness, compassion, gentleness, gratefulness, appreciation. "It is in reality love. And what is love? Love is God."[16]

Whether you are a Christian, Jew, or Muslim and the goal is to understand your heart is God, or you are a Buddhist and the goal is to know that your heart is your true Buddha nature, the point is the same. If you are completely secular and the goal is to understand that your heart is goodness, that is the same as well.

This is a very strange concept for us to wrap our heads around. We are not used to loving ourselves, let alone thinking of our heart as God.

But this truth stirs something within us and so we follow the path. We discover that our heart is light, love, compassion, humility, gratefulness, joy, contentment,

---

[16] This is not the God of your forefathers, the God in the heavens you prayed to. This is the God-essence within you.

strength, courage, and wisdom. With wisdom being the knowledge that our ego-mind is not our true self, to thus not identify with it, and instead see all things through the eyes of our unwounded heart, experiencing things directly without the intervention of thought.

To more completely connect with your true self, I encourage you to undertake this exercise. Imagine yourself in a dark room. And imagine finding your true self in that room; for me it was my smiling toddler. Say to it, "I'm coming home." See it reach it's hand out to you. Take that hand and let your true self lead you out of the dark room into the light.

Every time I am in some negative situation, and I feel that smiling toddler beside me and my hand in his, I feel his positive radiance course through me and outward. I am filled with light regardless what is happening around me. More on this in Chapter 3.

Before proceeding further, it is very important that you sit with what you've read here. Let it begin to bring a new clarity, a new awareness of who you are. And a way for you to understand why your life has been what it has been, not in a psychotherapeutic sense but in a macro-spiritual sense.

Feel the door open to loving yourself unconditionally and having compassion for yourself, knowing that the "you" that you have not loved and not had compassion for is not your true self; it is the product of your ego mind. Identify instead with your unwounded heart, your God/Buddha essence.

Your ego-mind will always remain part of you, but it will no longer control you. And despite the suffering it has caused, you will learn to have compassion for it because you understand how these feelings and perceptions formed and that they were not a product of free will choice.

To further tune your heart will require that you go deeper and remove the impediments to feeling your heart, being open to it. That is the subject of the next chapter. It will walk you through the process of freeing yourself from

the control of your feelings and perceptions, the control of your ego-mind.
    But first ...

3. And Our True Nature Is ... ?

In addition to your true self ... your heart, your God/Buddha essence ... you were also born with a temperament, a nature. This is not something that developed over time.

Your true nature has two aspects. The first is your temperament. This is not what we normally think of as personality; that is a function of your learned experience, your ego-mind. Your temperament is something you were born with. It is the essence of your nature. For example, if you look at the enlightened beings or holy men you have had some exposure to, they are all distinct people; they are not clones. They may all act from their heart but yet they are different. They have their own way of expressing themselves, of interacting with others.[17]

When you are unburdened of your ego-mind, when you have said "not me" to all the things that are your learned experience and not your true self (see Chapter 3), what you will be left with is your true personality, your temperament.

The other aspect of your true nature is the thing, something deep within you, that drives you. Some people may be born artists, some may be born tinkerers, some may be born gardeners, some may be born thinkers.

This is not to be confused with innate talents. For example, I can with modesty say that I have musical talent; I have composed worthy pieces of music. But as much as I loved doing that and derived great satisfaction from it, I would not say that I am an artist. Rather I am artistic. To be an artist is to be driven by your very nature to express yourself through art. I was not driven in that way; instead I was driven by a desire to memorialize my deceased partner.

Another way of looking at the difference between true nature and talent is something Bette Davis once said in an interview. She said that if you have to ask other people

---

[17] See my book, *The Self in No Self*

whether you should be an actress or are good enough to be an actress, then you're not meant to be an actress. If being an actress is in your nature, you know it with every fiber of your body; there is no doubt, no thinking about it.

Everyone ... regardless their intelligence level, their status in life ... has something in their true nature that they are meant to do. Note that this does not involve achieving anything ... that would be the ego-mind attaching itself to your true nature. There is no craving. There is no lack of equanimity. It just involves doing, trying, expressing.

So many of us go through life with nothing driving us other than the desire to make more money, to please others, to be acknowledged. There is nothing from within that drives us and therefore nourishes us. That is why so many people don't like their jobs. Forgetting about all the other problems people have in the workplace, their work does not connect with or give voice to their true nature.

It used to be that people had hobbies which often allowed them to give voice to their true nature. It was a respite from their job. But now very few have time for hobbies. Everybody is busy even outside of work. We have lost sight of what life is about.

Think about yourself. Has there been a recurring voice within you saying, "I would love to be/do ...?" But your sensible self or someone else said, "No, it's not practical," or "No, it's not the right time." Find a way to do it.

Again, as an example, I knew someone who all her life wanted to sing. She didn't want to be a "singer," a professional. She didn't even have a particularly good voice. But she always wanted to express herself through singing, and when she sang it did something for her. It was the only activity where she felt she was expressing herself, her feelings. Nevertheless she never followed through with this desire.

Finally at age 51 she decided she was going to do this and started taking singing lessons. She wanted to learn how to use her voice as best she could. Again, it wasn't about being successful or accomplished. It was just about trying, putting forth the effort. And that brought her joy.

Everyone has something in their true nature that drives them to express itself. To be in touch with that force, to give voice to it while not attaching to it, not craving it ... and this is a critical caveat ... would make every life more meaningful and fulfilling, and joyful. But succumb to your ego-mind's attempt to turn your desire into a craving and you will instead end up frustrated and you will suffer.

Chapter 3:
Freeing Your Self

It is one thing to know that your ego-mind is not your true self and that your true self is your heart. It is quite another thing to be able to free yourself from the control of your ego-mind.

Before we begin this process, it's necessary to again be clear why you are doing this. There is nothing you value more than your peace and happiness. And because you know your feelings and perceptions cause you suffering you need to be free of their control in order to experience peace and happiness with any consistency.

Reaffirm these truths and state your intent that you will allow *nothing* to disturb your peace and happiness.

Why is this step in the process so important? As I've said and as you've certainly experienced, your feelings and perceptions are very powerful and deeply rooted. They cannot be easily set aside.

Affirming these truths and assuming this attitude, this intent, will give you the will and discipline to stand up to your emotions and perceptions. Otherwise, your heart may want to do something, but your emotions will prevent you from proceeding. And once you are in the grip of your emotions, in their vortex, one is generally incapable of exercising good judgment or act in your best interest.

In beginning the process of freeing yourself, it is important to ask the question, "What is freedom?" Many people think that freedom is the ability to do whatever you want to do ... to have the money or power to obtain whatever your ego-mind and our culture tells you you need. That is certainly how the ego-mind looks at freedom.

But if you follow what your ego-mind tells you to do, then you are not really free; you are instead in the control of a force other than your true self. You are chained to the past. *True freedom is being free of the control of your ego-mind, your feelings and perceptions, so that you really have a choice, true free will, to do what is in your best interest, to follow your heart.*

My statement about "free will" may well raise an eyebrow. We live in a culture in which both the secular and religious codes are based in large part on the assumption that we have free will. That we have the ability to choose right from wrong. That we have the ability to choose to do something or not.

But in reality most of us only operate within a very narrow range of free will. Each of us has been programmed by our life experiences to think, respond, and act in a particular way. Our concept of right and wrong depends very much on those experiences. Our ability to act, or perhaps more frequently not act, is very much circumscribed by that programming.

When I use the word "programmed" I mean it both in a physiological and a computer sense. Let me explain.

When we are born, our brain is pretty much a blank slate. At around age 3, we begin forming feelings, perceptions, thoughts that go to the brain; what are called "synapses" are formed. Synapses are the way that one cell communicates with another; it forms a pathway. The more frequently we react to an experience in the same way, the stronger the pathway. And so our ego-mind is formed. If you will, it's as though an internal programming code has been written to control how or if we act and how we feel about ourselves. By the time most of us begin to question our ego-mind, these pathways have become deeply ingrained. Despite the incredible human brain and its potential, we humans act in ways which are almost robotic.

That is why I say so often that the roots of our feelings and perceptions run deep and that it is very difficult to free ourselves from the control of our ego-mind. It's not just that we've been acting this way all our lives, that we're seeking to alter a paradigm that's developed over a lifetime, it's that physiologically we have been programmed to react to experiences in certain ways.

That is why if one thinks one can re-train your ego-mind ... which many people do ... one will be hitting a brick wall. Instead, the effort here is to establish new synapses, new ways to react to experiences that come from your heart, your true self.

The purpose of this book, and any spiritual path, is to enable you to free yourself from this internal programming, from the control of your feelings and perceptions, your habit-energies, so that you indeed experience free will. Bit by bit as you work through this book, you will be looking to your heart not your ego-mind for guidance; bit by bit you will be creating and strengthening new synapses, thus slowly turning your will and your life over to the care of your true self, your heart and freeing yourself from the control of your ego-mind.

When we are able to experience things directly, free of our emotions and labels, free of the intervention of our ego-mind, then we will be able to see things clearly. Only then can we make decisions on what to think or how to act based on the guidance of our heart, not our emotions.

For most of us, this is uncharted territory. And so, many are stopped in their tracks by their fear or distrust of the unknown, in this case their heart. Instead we continue to react to things the way we are used to and feel comfortable with ... reacting based on our emotions. We feel secure in these habit-energies regardless how much suffering we know they bring

This is a perfect example of fear holding us back from doing something that is in our best interest. It's understandable that we experience this fear. But we must free ourselves from its control if we are to experience peace and happiness. As the old saying goes, "We have nothing to fear but fear itself."

FINDING INNER PEACE

After sitting with the thoughts expressed in the previous chapter, you hopefully have come to understand that you have no reason to fear turning your will over to the care of your heart because your heart would never hurt you. While on the other hand you have clarity that your emotions and perceptions, your cravings and attachments, are the cause of your suffering.

Most importantly, you have hopefully come to identify with your heart, your God/Buddha essence and know that your ego-mind is not your true self. This is critical because to the extent that you still identify with your ego-mind and its emotions, it will make it that much harder to perform the steps outlined in this chapter in a meaningful way.

In this chapter, I will discuss essential steps or techniques to use to free yourself. As with other parts of this book, it is important that you not just read and nod your head. It is important that you stop and think, absorb what you are reading, think about how it applies to you and your life, and imagine what it would be like if you followed the advice I present rather than react with your habit-energy.

FREEING YOUR SELF

1. Form the Intent to Change Your Reaction to Things, to Not Let Anything Disturb Your Peace and Happiness

The serenity prayer says, "Lord, grant me the strength to accept the things I cannot change (which is the way my life is right now) and the courage to change the things I can (which is how I relate to myself and the world around me ... the thoughts I think, the words I speak, and the actions I take). That really comes pretty close to the essence of all spiritual teaching on how to end suffering.

The most difficult part is changing our reactions to ourselves and the world around us. You've gone through the process of learning that all of your feelings and perceptions ... all your emotions, judgments, attachments, cravings ... are a product of your ego-mind. They are not a function of your true self, your heart. Further, you have learned the truth that it is your feelings and perceptions, not the facts of your life experience, that cause your suffering. And you have begun the process of connecting with and knowing your heart.

But that understanding, while somewhat reducing the power of your feelings and perceptions, your habit-energies, does not free you from their control. Other steps are required.

I've said it earlier and I'm sure I'll say it again ... never underestimate the force and cunning of your ego-mind. Its habit-energies have formed our identity and how we have thought about our place in the world for our entire life; they are thus deeply ingrained. Now we are seeking the courage to stand up to our emotions and perceptions because they cause us suffering, they disturb our peace and happiness.

The first step is to form the intent to change your various reactions, to not let anything disturb your peace and happiness. This is not a global process; one must be aware and have the intent to change each and every reaction you have. One might think, "No big deal," but forming such an intent requires great clarity and discipline because it goes against the grain of your life.

To form this intent you have to have deep faith ... in your true self being your heart. And that all will be well regardless what life throws your way because you will always return home to your heart, your God/Buddha-essence and be at peace and happy. Without this faith, your fear will prevent you from forming the intent.

The other thing necessary is that you be aware when a particular reaction disturbs your peace and happiness. Initially you will know there are things that obviously are problems and you will form the intent to change those reactions. But as time passes, you will discover that you keep becoming aware of more things that disturb you. It's quite amazing just how many things we do habitually, without thought, that disturb our peace and happiness. And as you become aware of each, you will form a new intent regarding that reaction.

But once you have formed the intent, you then have to have the will-power to carry it out. One morning while meditating, I thought about my past experiences and realized that to have that will-power to stand up to your ego-mind you need a "motivator."

One would think that the desire to end your suffering, to experience peace and happiness, would in and of itself be a sufficient motivator. But that would underestimate the force of your ego-mind. It is only sufficient where the ego is not very threatened.

For matters that go more to the core of your ego, there has to be a more powerful motivator to give us the will to say "no" to our ego-mind. I have experienced such a motivator in several forms.

One motivator was knowing that my habit reactions caused someone I loved much suffering, much agitation. For example, I would express righteous indignation when I got angry at certain things or people, which caused him to suffer because it surrounded him with a very negative energy that

FREEING YOUR SELF

dragged him down.[18] Or I did some things habitually which seemed very benign and even helpful to me, but they again caused him much suffering because they robbed him of his strength and self-confidence.[19] Because of my love for him, and only because of that love, I formed the will, the intent, to change my way of reacting to or relating to certain things. And I did in fact change.

Another motivator was hitting rock bottom, a very dark space. This was the case with my addiction. I certainly had tried to end my addiction many times over the years, to exercise self-control. But it was only when I really hit rock bottom that I had the will-power to form an intent and implement it to save myself. This is why so many people who are addicts relapse after short periods of sobriety ... they have not hit rock bottom. Even then it was a hard and long process, and still I will always be a recovering addict; it is always there, lurking.

But as with all things spiritual, it is not enough to identify the habit-energies you need to let go. You need to replace the void created with something positive and truthful. Otherwise, the ego will just come rushing back in to fill the void.

In the first case I described, it was helpful to replace my habit-energy reaction to things with this truth: things are the way they are because it's just the way it is.

Early in my practice, I met a traveling American Theravadan monk. He had spent years in the jungles of Thailand and was fearless. At one point, I asked him why, if we are all born essentially perfect, suffering is the common

---

[18] The reader may wonder why this went to the core of my ego. Behind this indignation was the feeling that I was smarter, better than the mass of others; this had been one of my main coping mechanisms for feeling rejected by many of my peers.

[19] This went to the core of my ego not because I desired to offer joy ... that comes from my heart ... but because I felt that if I weren't able to help people, be useful, I would not be needed and loved.

human experience. His answer was, "It's just the way it is. It's like the law of thermodynamics."

When I heard his words a huge burden was lifted from my shoulders. While acceptance was still key to achieving peace and serenity, that acceptance was made easier by understanding that things are the way they are because it's just the way it is. It had nothing to do with me personally. Even if something did still have a negative label in my mind, it wasn't really for me to accept; it just *was*.

More recently though I've come to understand another aspect of the wisdom of "it's just the way it is." It's not only about understanding that things are the way they are because that's just the way it is, it's about viewing things free of thought, not placing any value judgments on what we observe or experience based on our learned experience.

Again, to be clear, this does not mean that I let life roll over me, that I am not concerned about things or work to change things; I am very aware. But it does mean that I don't get agitated by things. Which actually frees me to exercise good judgment and be productive.

And so at first, my use of the phrase "it's just the way it is" generally arose in a negative context. I didn't like the way things were, I didn't approve of what was happening, but I said to myself, "it's just the way it is," and I accepted that fact. I wasn't happy about it, but I accepted it. Actually, when I had reason to use this practice, it always was within a negative context; if I was happy with things there was no reason to resort to, "it's just the way it is."

Now I understand that the deeper meaning of this practice is experiencing things directly without the intervention of thought, without any judgment or labels. And so it has changed from a statement of resignation, something I resorted to as a coping mechanism, to a positive statement about my relationship with all things.

In the case of my addiction, I replaced my habit energy with a belief in my true self, my heart, my Buddha nature. I was not some weak creature who resorted to degrading behavior to escape the world he feared. I was my heart, which was strong and filled with light and love. I had no need to resort to illicit pleasures in order to distract my mind from reality.

Having formed the intent to change your habit-energy reaction to things and having replaced your former way of thinking with a truth, you now have to implement your intent. By finding a motivator, you develop the necessary willpower to do that. But it still doesn't happen automatically. So how do you not fall back into your habit-energy?

2. "Not me!" - Peeling Off the Layers of Our Ego-Mind

The first thing you must do is to disown your feelings and perceptions as being part of your true self. They are part of your ego-mind, but not your heart.

Another teaching uses the term, "purge," to describe this process. To me though that phrase has a violence and ruthlessness to it, and violence should not be part of the process. It instead should be a gentle process; one should always be gentle with oneself, gentle but firm. Also "purge" means to get rid of. And as I've explained, the purpose of walking the path is not to get rid of your emotions and perceptions, but rather not to be controlled by them.

The Vietnamese Zen monk, Huyen Te, whose teaching I received for many years, told how he would name his various feelings and perceptions and say, "Not me!" while simultaneously flipping his arm up, flicking his wrist, and snapping his fingers. I adopted this practice as well. It is very direct, firm, yet gentle, even light-hearted.

What I found, though, is that the process is not quite so simple. First, you cannot say, "Not me!" regarding some subset of feelings and perceptions and have that negation apply globally to all your feelings and perceptions. Each individual feeling and perception must be sat with so you are focused on that particular feeling/perception, know that it does not flow from your heart, but have compassion for why it is part of your ego-mind.

This will require a good amount of introspection, best practiced during meditation. For example, a number of years ago, an incident occurred that brought out the satisfaction that I still felt at being right. I had been talking with a friend about something and thought I saw what the reality was and so said that he and others hadn't gotten it right. He called me on it, and it was deserved.

I then sat with the satisfaction I got from being right. What was this all about? At first, I located this habit-energy in the experience during 19 years of schooling of being rewarded for being right, by getting good grades. That's how you got a gold star. That's how you were valued.

But as I continued to sit I was aware that that answer did not go deep enough. The reason why I craved to be rewarded and valued is that I craved respect. And I craved respect because as a child I did not feel loved by my father and thought I was not lovable or worthy of love. I also felt unwanted by many of my peers. Gaining respect was my substitute for love, both from my father and from my peers.

Yet I knew that these feelings were just a product of my mind. And my practice of tonglen on myself had allowed me to see that in truth I was always loved by my father and have always been valued by him and many others. And so I said to this craving, "Not me!"

Often, though, it will be the case that your feelings are not based on a misperception, your imagination. But nevertheless you will know that your reactions to these experiences, these emotions, don't flow from your heart and so you will say, "Not me!"

Again, these feelings will always be part of my ego-mind. And I have great compassion for them and understand why they formed. But I know they do not flow from my true self.

This practice alone, when done regularly, will help change your paradigm. It will weaken the control of your ego-mind. But it is just a step. More needs to be done. So read on.

3. Discovering the Truth from Within

It is one thing to intellectually understand that your feelings and perceptions are just a product of your mind, a product of your learned experience, and to disown them as not part of your true self. It will enable you to make significant progress on your path.

But to progress to the next stage, it is necessary to discover from within that indeed your feelings and perceptions are just a product of your mind and therefore have no inherent reality. They sure feel real, but they are not.

Let me use my relationship with the emotion of fear as an example. Fear is one of the most controlling feelings that we have. It can physically incapacitate us. Psychologically, it can tie us in knots. What was once a primal reaction to danger, a protector, has in man become a major source of suffering and an inhibitor of clear thinking and action.

To help free ourselves from fear, we are taught that fear is a product of the mind. And we learn from the Buddha, as I've related, that because fear and the other emotions and perceptions cause suffering, they are not us, they are not ours, they are not our selves, because our selves would not cause us such suffering.

These lessons were all very helpful in my efforts to disengage myself from fear and the other emotions. Yet fear was so deeply embedded in me that it nevertheless remained strong and carried me off with some, although less frequent, regularity into its negative world-perspective. Even after years of meditation practice. Even after years of saying, "Not me!" Until relatively recently.

One morning a few years ago, I woke up and fear sank its claws into me with my first thought and would not let go until, as a defensive measure, I started singing a cheerful song in my mind and the fear disappeared. When I sat down to meditate, fear was on top of me again. It was actually scary; I felt I was losing it. But as I focused on my breathing, the sounds around me, and the point in front of me, and became present, the fear disappeared again.

I realized then, at that very moment, that I had just been given proof that fear is just a product of the mind. If fear had an existence independent of the mind, I would still have felt fear when singing the song or when I concentrated and was present.

But since I couldn't experience both fear and another mind-activity, such as singing or being present, at the same time, and since the mind cannot be in two places at the same time, it follows that fear must be just a product of the mind. (Many people think that the mind can be in two places at the same time, but really what happens is that the mind switches back and forth between subjects instantaneously, so the break isn't noticed.)

Compare this with the experience of physical pain. Whether I'm singing a song or meditating and present, if I experience physical pain, I will feel it. Such pain is real, it is not a product of the mind.

Since that day, I can honestly say that I have not been controlled by my fears. They have arisen from time to time, they are still part of me, but weakened. And so I have been able to say, "no, I'm not going there" to them and return to my heart and my faith that in truth all will be well regardless what life throws my way because I will always return home to my unborn Buddha mind and so be at peace and happy.

Epiphanies happen unbidden, whether during meditation or upon waking up or really any point during the day. It can happen early in your process of walking the path or it can happen after years.

The point is that if you are disciplined in your practice they will come. And when they do, when you discover the truth from within rather than just know it intellectually, it will have a major impact on your ability to find inner peace on a sustained basis.

4. Change Your Reaction to Things

Once you have formed the intent to not let anything disturb your peace and happiness, and you have said "Not me!" to your various feelings and perceptions, and you have discovered from within a core truth, you would think that would do it. You would be set to experience peace and happiness.

Not quite. That certainly breaks the hardest ground, tilling the soil as it were, but you need to take the next and critical step of actually implementing your intent by changing how you react to yourself and the world around you. All the while remembering this truth: suffering is not caused by what happens to you, it is caused by how you react to what happens to you.

There are several techniques you should use to surmount the remaining barriers created by your ego-mind ... the barriers may be lower because of the work you've done, but they're still there and can be formidable. This will enable you to implement your intent to change the way you habitually react to things, to be at peace and happy.

The techniques are: Imagining reacting differently as part of your meditation. Opening your heart to embrace all aspects of your being and experience. And testing and rejecting harmful guidance, guidance that urges you to do something or think in a way likely to bring you suffering rather than peace and happiness.

<u>Imagining Reacting Differently</u>

During a dharma discussion at a Shambhala center, part of the reading mentioned using imagination as part of the meditation process ... imagine something specific happening that would normally upset you and "see" how you could react to the situation differently in a spiritual way. The idea is to prepare yourself for the eventuality.

When I first heard this, it seemed a bit odd as it

sounded the opposite of being present. But during a meditation several days later, I decided to incorporate this with regard to a situation that was coming up and which might be somewhat upsetting if I wasn't aware. The situation was that I was going to be seeing some people who I felt had slighted me.

I imagined various scenarios and saw how I would habitually respond and how I could instead respond spiritually by understanding that the action that was upsetting was an expression of the other person's suffering. It had nothing to do with me. Also, I saw myself entering the group more joyfully, with a heart-felt wish that everyone experience happiness. As a result, in this imagining I felt no slight and felt one with the group.

When the event actually happened, I followed through on my meditation's imagining. I purposefully approached the group joyfully, my interactions with people were thus different, and people responded. When I saw people who I felt had slighted me in the past, I saw that their action was an expression of their suffering and felt no more slight and only wanted happiness for them. There was one person towards whom I initially had a somewhat critical judgmental reaction, but I caught myself and turned that around to compassion.

So the imagining process definitely altered my actual experience of the event. It both removed my value judgment of their actions and changed my reaction. The result was that I was at peace and happy. I have since used this technique repeatedly.

I know it must sound strange or even troubling that someone who is as seriously into their practice as I am, who has been doing it for more than 20 years, and who has made much meaningful progress on the path still is beset with the types of challenges which I openly relate here and in my blogposts.[20]

---

[20] www.thepracticalbuddhist.com

But that is a function of living in this world. Life is a constant challenge no matter how far along the path one is. And it's a constant challenge not because the world is in fact so dysfunctional, but because our ego-mind and its habit-energies are so deeply rooted. Be compassionate towards yourself. Walking the path is not about perfection; it's about having the right intent and always trying.

One can only do the best one can. And as the years go by, one is rewarded with ever-more moments, hours, and days of peace and happiness.

The Heart's Embrace

Despite having freed myself from my emotions, including the biggest one - fear, I cannot say that I felt happy. I was calm, at peace, nothing agitated me, but I did not feel happy as a general rule. I experienced joy, but that was momentary.

I still felt that there was a gray cloud always hanging over me. Besides the fact that I just didn't feel happy, the other evidence that indeed I wasn't was that the default position of my facial muscles was a perpetual frown.

I had tried various methods to change this, but nothing had worked except momentarily. When I did Thich Nhat Hanh's "mouth yoga" and brought a smile purposefully to my face, or when I would be out and purposefully emanate loving kindness and feel a smile on my face, I did feel lighter, freer. But those remedial efforts had just a temporary effect.

My "Not me!" practice hadn't worked because, as I noted earlier, that practice does not work globally; each individual feeling or perception must be sat with. Well, my malaise/seriousness/moroseness ... whatever you want to call it ... was not on my list of things to disown. I thought it was just the way I was ... would you believe! At that time, I had not yet connected with my heart and the joy of my smiling toddler.

Several years later, a friend told me about a teaching he

had come across that encouraged opening your heart to embrace all aspects of yourself, including your dark side. He noted that I often seemed caught up in trying to free myself from various "problems" and that I should try this practice of embracing them instead. I knew this was certainly consistent with the teaching of Pema Chodron and others.

And so when I next meditated, I sat with my heart and I felt it embrace all aspects of my being, including my weaknesses, my dark side, my moroseness, my wounded inner child. As I did this I hugged myself. The experience was cathartic, with tears streaming down my face.

Notice that I did not say that "I" embraced all aspects of my being and experience, instead my heart, my true self, did this. My ego-mind would never embrace all aspects of my being and experience. Only my heart, my true self, will do that and free me.

An important part of changing how we react to things, to opening up our heart, is to increase our identification with our heart, to turn our will and our lives over to its care. To let go our ego's desire to control everything.

This is difficult for us because the ego is so strong and it is our habitual way of life. This despite the fact that we have come to know we suffer endlessly from the urgings of our ego-mind but understand instinctively that our heart would never do anything to harm us.

Because the issue underlying my malaise/frown is something that so many people suffer from, let me discuss the particulars of my history further in the hope that this may be helpful.

The Sufi have developed a chart of nine personality types (the enneagram) and the "false core beliefs" that underlie each of the nine. "These beliefs reflect the conclusions about ourselves we came to as the result of our early childhood traumas or experiences."[21]

When I read the nine false core beliefs, I knew which

---

[21] Charlotte Kasl, *What if the Buddha Dated*, Penguin Compass, 1999

one was mine, "There must be something wrong with me." In one way, this was not a revelation to me because I have been aware for many years that this belief had a major negative impact on my childhood and life. But it was a revelation in that I now understood why I did not feel happy despite all the progress I had made on the path and why my face had been in a perpetual frown. I had not "connected the dots."

This false core belief was so deeply embedded in my ego that no matter how far my spiritual practice had come, it still controlled the overall ambiance of my persona. Thus I always felt there was some grayness surrounding me.

When I was fighting my perpetual frown and trying to rid myself of it, it only made this false core belief stronger. As the ancient Chinese poem "Affirming Faith in Mind" says, "seek rest and no rest comes instead."

But opening up my heart to embrace all aspects of my being took this aspect of my psyche which was so deep it was in my bones and removed all internal struggle. It in effect smothered these negative feelings with love. I was made whole.

As a further result of opening my heart to embrace all aspects of my being and experience,[22] I for the first time knew from within myself the truth of Pema Chodron's teaching that we have everything we need inside ourselves to be happy and at peace because we don't need anything to be a specific way to be at peace and happy; I had embraced everything, nothing needed to change. Free of internal struggle I felt at peace and happy; that is my natural state.

Only we can take that state away from ourselves. And by implication, we have the power to give it back to ourselves. I felt an undefined faith and trust. And because I was one with my heart, I felt strong. And I smiled.

---

[22] I added "experience" because I knew that to free myself from suffering I had to embrace all my life experience, not just my being. It all just happened, it was, no labels.

Please note that, as with all practices, this is not a once and done thing. You need to come back to and implement the heart's embrace regularly, if not daily. It will be a fundamental underpinning for your inner peace.

My life was truly transformed by this meditation. Nothing that I have experienced since has agitated me, has pushed my buttons. I am aware and experience things directly and dispassionately, free of labels. And because I have found happiness from within, my face is no longer set in a perpetual frown. (Occasionally, yes, but not perpetually.)

Testing and Rejecting Harmful Guidance

By now you understand that regardless how much you practice, how far you've come, one must always be vigilant regarding your ego-mind. It will seize any moment of weakness or distraction as an opportunity to gain the upper hand in the conflict between light and darkness, between your heart and your ego-mind. Any or all of your feelings and perceptions will likely continue to rise and attempt to lead you astray. And so none of these techniques I've discussed is a once and done thing; they just be part of your practice every day.

For this reason, the next technique I will discuss must always be at hand: testing the wisdom of the guidance you receive and rejecting it if harmful. You must always test the wisdom of what you're doing or thinking of doing.

Although more of your guidance may be coming from your heart, it is probable that much of your guidance is still coming from your ego-mind. Here again it is necessary to turn this testing over to your heart, your true self; your ego-mind will never reject it's own advice.

You cannot just ask whether the guidance is coming from you heart or your mind. Why? Because the ego-mind is so sly and has so many forms that what you think is coming from your heart or your inner self may really just be your ego-mind in disguise.

And so you must hold up each guidance to a test of dependable clarity to determine whether it is right for you. And if it is not right, reject it and seek guidance from your heart.

And what is this dependable test? It's very simple ... once you've gone through the process of asking yourself what is most important to you, what you value most, as set forth in Chapter 1. That process will always end with the inner self-truth that peace and happiness is what you value most.

So this is the test: if a guidance brings you peace and happiness, it is right for you. But if it brings you agitation and suffering, it is not right for you.

In the latter instance, either the thought/action itself is disruptive and you need to stop, or you are approaching an otherwise appropriate desire or feeling from an unskillful perspective, from a lack of equanimity, in which case you have to find a way to approach it with equanimity, free of emotion.

To show you how this actually works, let's return to the two examples I gave in Chapter 1. In the first, our appropriate desire to make friends becomes an obsession, which creates anxiety and fear. Why? Because we are insecure, we feel unwanted, we need the approval or attention of others to feel happy. The antidote to these feelings and the door to equanimity is to perform the practice "Not me!" regarding these feelings.

How might that actually look? "I'm aware of the suffering caused by feeling insecure, that I need something outside myself or something inside me needs to change to be happy, and yet I know that this feeling is just a product of my mind, and so I say to it, 'Not me!' And in truth my true self is secure because I know that I have everything I need inside myself to be at peace and happy and accept my life as it is right now at this moment. Nothing needs to change."

FREEING YOUR SELF

In addition to the "Not me!" practice, open up your heart and embrace all aspects of your being and experience ... your insecurity, your rejection by others, your feeling unwanted, your feeling something's wrong with you ... so all internal struggles regarding these feelings and experiences will cease.

The combination of these two practices will allow you to approach your desire to make friends with equanimity. To say to yourself, "If it happens, great. If it doesn't happen, that's ok too."

Regarding the second example of being hurt by something that was said or done to you and reacting with anger and resentment. The first requirement is that you have the intent of freeing yourself from the control of your anger. That may sound like a "duh!" statement, but believe me it isn't.

Once you're past that, the process is similar in that you say "Not me!" regarding those emotions; they are a product of your mind not your heart. And then you open your heart to embrace those emotions. Again this does not mean to give way to them but rather to accept your anger as something that's there and will always be there. It's ok. It's understandable. Have compassion towards it. But don't give voice to it.

A further step to achieving equanimity in this situation is to develop compassion for those who hurt you, remembering that anything that pushes your buttons is a direct result of the other person's suffering. They did not make a choice to hurt you; it's just the way they are, the way they've been programmed by their life experiences.

But for those hurts that provoke overwhelming resentment and anger ... often concerning family members because there is a sense of betrayal ... these techniques, even in combination, may not free you. To a large extent because our ego-mind really doesn't want us to be free of these emotions. We are very self-righteous about our anger.

Because anger and resentment are so powerful and

destructive, second only probably to fear, and are so common, I thought I would address this situation more fully.

One day while meditating I realized that a major reason why we feel resentment is because at the time of the experience we felt unable to defend ourselves, to speak out against what happened. Whether we feared the loss of love, a job, or whatever, we felt we didn't have the power to protect ourselves by speaking.

The way to break this negative energy and to regain equanimity is to finally speak, to communicate directly with those involved ... in a way that will achieve the related goals of both feeling you have defended yourself and freeing yourself from this negative emotion. The right way to speak (whether orally or in writing) involves several components.

First, be very clear what the truth is. You must separate what actually happened from the spin you have put on it over the years. As the saying goes, "The facts, nothing but the facts." But don't go into all the gory details, just enough to make your point. Second, state clearly but free of emotion how the incident impacted you, whether in a practical way or emotionally. Third, place this statement of truth in the context of compassion, both towards yourself and the other person(s). Explain that your need to finally speak the truth and free yourself from this negative energy is having compassion for yourself. You show compassion towards the other by stating what happened free of emotion and recognizing explicitly that what occurred was the result of the other's suffering ... no one voluntarily chooses to be nasty.

In working through this process, you may discover two related things. First, that the hurt you experienced was part of a systematic abuse of you by a parent or sibling and that while angry you were in denial about the purposefulness of their actions; you just couldn't face the horrific truth. Now you know that they, like many other parents/siblings, were psychologically damaged and so purposefully went about hurting you.

Second, that because you couldn't accept that your parent or sibling was doing this to you purposefully ... you were after all desperate for their love ... you blamed yourself, felt that you were in some way guilty for what happened. You also blamed yourself and felt guilt and shame for not taking any action and thus being complicit in what happened. Which in turn made you all the more angry and resentful.

You heal yourself from the first of these realizations by understanding that it had nothing to with you; it was all about them and their psychopathological behavior. By speaking the truth with compassion, you have already let all of this go. Your heart longs for peace; it is your mind that wants to obsess about your abuse and have revenge.

Healing yourself from the second realization, that you felt guilt or shame, involves healing your inner child and thus healing your wounded heart. This is a major issue that lies hidden for many people, including myself until quite recently. It is an essential part of the process of finding inner peace. See the next section.

Once you have spoken ... *if* you speak as I've suggested, not with hateful passion ... you will find that you feel greatly relieved. The festering pain and resulting anger will be gone.

Replacing your mind's anger will be your heart's sadness. Because this isn't about forgetting; you will still feel hurt. And sadness is an expression of compassion by your heart for that hurt. As a result, your peace will no longer be disturbed by the past experience. You will have achieved equanimity.

From that position of sadness and equanimity, you will be ready to forgive. Remember that you forgive to heal yourself, to give yourself peace; it's not for the other person. It's having compassion towards yourself. Also, forgiveness does not absolve the other person of responsibility for what happened; your speaking the truth makes that clear. (See my blogpost, "The Stages of Forgiveness."[23])

In testing your guidance, rejecting it if it harms you, and finding equanimity, always hold your intent to not let anything disturb your peace and happiness in the forefront of your mind, knowing that nothing is more important to you. Nothing that your ego-mind presses upon you ... and it will press upon you ... is more important. Do not allow *anything* to disturb your peace and happiness. It is your birthright.

This sounds very straight-forward, which it is. But in order for you to practice this technique consistently, you must not only be unwavering in the importance to you of peace and happiness, you must be present.

If you are not present in the moment, if you are not aware when the ego-mind arises, it will take control and it will be off and running, dragging you behind it, before you know what's happening. And once you're in its vortex, it's almost impossible to stop until you drop, exhausted by the emotion. This will provide a teachable moment, but what you really want is to not go there, to not suffer.

None of us are aware 24/7. Our minds wander, we're distracted; it's the nature of the beast. Perhaps if one is enlightened this doesn't happen, but I wouldn't count on it. I assume that's one reason why even enlightened ones meditate hours every day. Clearly though, you and I have not reached that exalted state.

So, how do we increase our awareness? This is a constant challenge of vital importance. The best way to increase our moments of awareness throughout the day is to periodically stop and create an inner quiet space, regardless where we are or what we're doing.

One can create that space by watching one's breathing, by chanting, or by visualizing something that for you is very peaceful (I visualize that photo of me as a smiling toddler that I saw as my true Buddha self). More on this in the next

---

[23] www.thepracticalbuddhist.com

chapter.

    Just practicing any of these techniques for a moment or two will re-center you, bring you back home to your heart and the present. This will increase your level of awareness even after you go on with your day, making it more likely that when your ego-mind arises, you will know it.

5. Healing Your Inner Child - Healing Your Wounded Heart

As a child or adolescent we were all wounded by life experiences, by the world around us. We were hurt in countless ways, including being made to feel we are guilty or shameful, bad.

Those feelings have remained bottled up within us, festering, because as a child we had no one to talk to about those feelings. It is a rare parent that says to their child, "I want you to talk to me about anything that upsets you. It doesn't matter what it is. I am here for you. I love you. I will help you." Instead the child feels he or she cannot tell their parents what they feel because they fear the parent will be hurt, disappointed, or disgusted.

And so, in response to these life experiences, our ego-mind develops a variety of emotions, judgments, cravings, and attachments, as well as denial, to "protect" us. Which instead just cause us endless frustration and suffering. This is the world of your wounded inner child.

You have discovered that your true self is your heart, your unwounded heart. And you have learned several techniques to free yourself from the control of your ego-mind, enabling you to listen and follow the guidance of your heart and thus end your suffering.

But as I've previously related, despite this work having enabled me to experience peace on a consistent basis, I was not experiencing happiness on a consistent basis. Yes, I experienced more happiness since practicing the heart's embrace. And when I experienced a grayness, a blahness, I was able to effectively counter it by conjuring up the image of my smiling toddler that I see as my true Buddha self. But I sensed that all was still not quite right. The norm should be happiness, not blahness.

Then recently I learned of a technique I had never heard of before ... healing your inner child. From listening to others and now from my own experience, I believe this

FREEING YOUR SELF

practice is key to removing the last barrier to experiencing both inner peace and happiness.

Why is this necessary after all the other things you've been taught to do to free yourself from the control of your ego-mind? Because you were wounded as a child, or as an adolescent. The work you have done so far is about how you as an adult relate to yourself and the world around you.

That is huge. But it doesn't heal your inner child, your wounded heart, and thus you still suffer ... sometimes in a quiet way as I have or it can be in a very powerful way; it depends on how bad the wound was.

Your wounded inner child is not just something from the past; it is alive within you now. Just as the smiling toddler is the avatar of your true self, so too your wounded inner child is the avatar of your ego-mind.

And so to find peace and happiness, to free yourself from the prison of your mind, you both have to be one with your true self, your heart, *and* heal your wounded inner child.

In healing the inner child, it is very important that you not just understand that your true self is your heart but that you have begun to identify with it. Because it is only your unwounded heart, your smiling toddler, that has the ability to heal your inner child.

Why? Because most of us, that is to say our ego-minds, don't usually have much compassion for the inner child. We think it has failed us; we feel it's guilty or are ashamed of it. We do not love our inner child unconditionally, if at all. Which is why we don't love ourselves. To heal our inner child, just like our adult selves, we must get past that barrier by identifying with our true self, our heart.

The process starts with practicing *tonglen* on yourself, as described earlier. Feel your true self, your smiling toddler, receive the suffering of your wounded inner child and send it unconditional love, compassion, faith, and trust. This unconditional embrace of your wounded inner child by your true self, your smiling toddler, is the core of the healing process. The two are like twins separated at birth; the time has come for them to find each other again.

Another exercise is to imagine your inner child in a dark room and suddenly your smiling toddler appears in the room. He reaches out his hand to your inner child, who takes it. And your smiling toddler leads your inner child out of the dark room into the light, out of the darkness of the world of the ego-mind into the light that is the natural state of the heart

Next, sit with your inner child and call on your spiritual mother and father (not the real ones!)[24] to come and nurture the child and give it the love and understanding that was most likely missing in his childhood. Feel the love and warmth radiating from them to your inner child. And feel your inner child respond to the love and warmth.

This won't bring about some magical transformation, but this part of the process is very important. Some of us grew up in very dysfunctional homes where we experienced no love or understanding. Even when there seemed to be an expression of love, it often really wasn't. But even for those of us, and I would include myself, who grew up in generally very loving homes, our parents were not there for us in the way we needed because our needs were greater than really any parent can provide.

Parents after all have their own problems and lives to deal with, which makes it impossible for them to be there for their child 100%. They have no intent to neglect or harm; they are just a product of and programmed by their life experiences just like everyone else. But each of us deserves total love, unconditional love, and so we now call on our spiritual parents to fill that void.

Next, ask your inner child what is wrong, what he's feeling. And let him or her speak whatever he comes up with; do not censor it. It will be the truth, regardless how

---

[24] Your spiritual mother and father can be totally imaginary or they can be real spiritual people you've come in contact with or heard in a video.

painful.

When the child speaks, say that it's ok to feel what he's feeling; it's natural, understandable. If he feels guilt or shame ... whether it's because of something he's done, what's been done to him, or his feeling complicit because he did not fight against it or tell his parents ... tell him that he's not a bad, shameful person. His heart is pure.

Tell him that if he was acted upon it was all about them and not him. He was a victim. Nor should he now question why he didn't protect himself, why he didn't run away, why he didn't speak up.

And if he did something wrong or hurt someone, well we all hurt people, even ourselves, at times. It's important to accept responsibility but that does not make us bad or shameful people.

Being hard on yourself is an ego-mind game. Your heart has nothing but compassion for you. You were a child who wanted to be loved and were in denial about the nature of what was happening to you. Your response was natural. A child reacts to events very differently than an adult would because children have a very narrow frame of reference; they are dependent; they're not aware of options.

In these healing exercises, the critical point is that you, your true self, open your heart to embrace your inner child and provide him/her with unconditional love. Give yourself and your inner child a hug. This is what was missing from your life as a child. And this can only come from your heart. Your ego-mind will seek justice or revenge, which may be seductive, but no healing will come from actions taken in response to those emotions.

Tell him or her that you are there for him, always. He is not alone. And that regardless what happened in the past, all will be well now because he is in a safe place surrounded by a loving you and by loving spiritual parents. This may not sound like much, but it's amazing the healing power of knowing that you are loved unconditionally and that someone will always be there for you.

What you hear may surprise you; it may scare you. But what you will hear is the truth. It was something that needed to come out, be spoken, in order for the healing process to take place.

As I noted earlier, children rarely feel they have the ability to speak the truth, to freely express their feelings. One of the common experiences of children is that they are not treated as "people;" they are not respected in that sense. Once children are past the toddler stage, parents rarely ask children what is wrong. And when they do, often it is with an almost accusing tone, not compassionate. They act impatient with their children. And so children often won't speak the truth; they are desperate for the love of their parents and won't risk offending them.

But it's not just your "child" that needs healing. When you grew up and passed through adolescence to young adulthood, you continued to be consumed by the negative images of yourself, the false core beliefs, that were impressed upon you as a child. And that young person suffered mightily. Go through the same process with him or her and the healing process will deepen.

If this seems like a lengthy process, it's because the wounds of your inner child run very deep. It is only through this loving practice that your inner child will be healed and your peace and happiness restored.

I have gone through this exercise myself and sat with both my inner child and my inner young man. This process will be ongoing, but already it has been transformative. Let me share my experience with you to give you a better understanding of the dynamic.

When I visited my inner child in his space, I called down my spiritual mother and father and they expressed unconditional love and understanding. My inner child responded, but one hug does not remove a lifetime of hurt.

When I asked my inner child what was wrong, he first told me that he didn't feel loved; he felt there was something wrong with him. Later he went deeper and said he felt insecure.

    I hugged him and said it was ok to feel those things, natural, understandable given what he experienced. But there is nothing wrong with him; he is a normal human, with strengths and weaknesses; and deep within his true self is his Buddha nature. Everyone feels insecure because of their life experiences. But I told him he was in a safe place now where he is loved unconditionally.

    The feelings he expressed were not a surprise to me. I have processed them previously, as I've written, using various techniques after understanding the truth that my true self was my heart, not my ego-mind. But clearly none of this helped my inner child who was still hurting. And so a different phase of the healing process had now begun.

    But when I sat with my inner young man (a teenager and college student), he spoke much to my surprise of the shame he felt regarding his same-sex sexual feelings and the secretive way he explored them. I say "surprised" because when I finally came out, I felt no shame, felt no internalized homophobia, because I was raised in a home where that was not present, where I knew my parents had had homosexual friends; I knew they would be accepting, and were. And I didn't remember feeling shame prior to that point.

    Obviously though when I was younger and had not come to terms with this, I felt very different; I guess I was in denial. And this affected me greatly. And so again, I hugged him and said that there was no reason to feel shameful about those sexual feelings. That was just the message from our culture. But in fact it's natural. And that I love him unconditionally and was there for him.

    Really what I was doing in both cases was being there for myself in a way I had never been before.

    The next few times I sat with my inner child, I wasn't expecting anything new (I had after all engaged in much introspection about my childhood). But I was surprised by his telling me about other things over which he felt guilt and shame, sometimes because of his felt complicity in not telling our parents about what happened.

I had never been aware of myself having feelings of guilt or shame about anything. I was not brought up with those feelings.

I was aware of the experiences/situations he mentioned, but I was not aware of having these negative feelings. They were suppressed and I was in denial. And so again I said to him that while it was natural for him to feel guilt and shame given the way children are conditioned, there was no real reason for him to have those feelings. He had done nothing wrong. He was not a bad person. I told him again that I loved him unconditionally and gave him a hug; and I encouraged him to hug himself.

It is too soon for me to feel the full benefits of this practice, but I sense that it will be transformative because I have opened myself up to being aware of and embracing feelings deep inside me. And that will change both the way I relate to myself and to those around me.

For example, when I meditated the morning after my initial inner child encounter, when I was at that part of my morning affirmations/mantras where I'm grateful for the love I've received in the past, including from my mother and father, and picture them and hear their voice, the experience went beyond mouthing the words, reminding myself. I felt love-energy flowing from both of them.

The experience really struck me and I wondered, why now. And I realized that by saying it was ok for me to feel as I felt, I was saying to everyone, including my parents, that it was ok to feel as they felt when they were growing up and that I therefore had compassion for the persons they had become. I always knew my mother loved me and I knew later in life that my father had always loved me. But when I recited my mantra, I never felt this particular energy flowing to me from them. I was now seeing them as they were, not as I wanted them to be and disappointed.

When I recently returned to my inner child/adolescent and asked how he was feeling, I was surprised to find him with a smile on his face, doing what he loved to do. He said that he felt loved unconditionally and was happy. To see and hear that was beyond heart-warming and I cried.

Sometime later, as I was exploring the mystery of memory, I went back to my childhood and revisited the most traumatic events, the things that have caused me so much suffering. Much to my surprise, I found that my inner child did not cry on these occasions. He was saddened, yes. But his strength was clear to me; it had been and was my ego-mind that was weak.

And it has been my ego-mind that focused, as the memory does, on these negative events and so they framed my "story." By trying to protect me, it obliterated the power of all the wonderful loving things I experienced, both as a child and later as an adult. I have been aware of those things but that awareness didn't change the story that I told myself about myself ... that I had an unhappy childhood and was unloved and unwanted. And so I suffered.

To free me from the blahness of that negative ambience, I realized I had to reclaim my story by literally rewriting it. I had to see my childhood and life as it really was, not as distorted by my ego-mind. And that I have done.

The process was empowering and heartwarming, putting my life back in perspective. Yes, I experienced trauma as a child that caused me suffering. But that was the doing of my ego-mind. On balance, I knew now that mine has been an overwhelmingly good life filled with much love and friendship. I felt a change within me. Whether it would last, whether I had freed myself from this aspect of the control of my ego-mind remained to be seen. But I was hopeful.

Sometimes the process of self-discovery never seems to end, so many are the layers of the ego-mind's feelings and perspectives. After reclaiming my story, I fully expected that my habitual frown would cease. Why else could I be frowning? I now knew my past was on balance loving; I was content in the present; and I knew that regardless what life threw my way in the future I would be ok, safe.

But my facial muscles did not relax. And so I asked, why? Then one morning while meditating the answer came to me in a flash of realization ... I had been subjected to Narc physical and mental abuse/attacks when I was a child and as an adult. To protect myself, my ego-mind had closed myself off from others; I erected a wall of protection that I only opened when I felt someone could be trusted. My facial muscles were habitually in a frown because I never knew when the next attack would come and so it was very difficult for me to truly relax and be present; and because I felt isolated.

Since most of you know nothing about Narcs, I need to back up and explain. Narcs are people with Narcissistic Personality Disorder (NPD), a mental condition recognized by the American Psychiatric Association's *Diagnostic and Statistical Manual of Mental Disorders*. They are evil, the devil incarnate. They have lost their humanity. One of the things they do is look for people who have the light, who are empaths, to either destroy them out of envy or steel their light. They are very similar to vampires.

When I had previously thought and written about these abusive experiences in my life, I had not made much of them. I knew they had been demeaning, humiliating, but I didn't understand their impact on me. I thought they occurred because I was different; it was because there was something wrong with me. Even when I began becoming familiar with the modus operandi of Narcs through a friend's research, I made no connection with my life.

But that morning it all fell into place and made sense. When I was a child, the smiling toddler I see in the photos of me, I was filled with light and joy. My father used to refer to me as "my sunshine." My mother wrote in my baby book that I was always in good humor; never a problem.

When I thought about how I came to lose this state of joy, I had contributed it mostly to problems I had with my father, feeling unloved by him. And secondarily, to feeling different from my peers and being treated differently by some. But now I know that while those experiences certainly had an impact, the primary negative impact on my life came from my reaction to those childhood abusive experiences.

Thus, despite all my spiritual work I was not able to shake off the discipline of not being open to people, to abandon my wall. I continued to be isolated in so many ways, whether it was not being friendly to wait staff or cashiers or not responding to people who approached me. I felt separated from others and I was on guard; this negativity enveloped my every moment.

I watched a video one night afterwards about how people of light can protect themselves from the psychic attack of Narcs or other predators. The answer is to always be in touch with the joy that is you, with the positive energy in your heart. That then creates a forcefield around you that no negativity can penetrate.

Interestingly, as I explain in the next section, when I first conjured up my smiling toddler and radiated loving-kindness to all, I felt like a forcefield was created that no negativity, no emotion from my ego-mind, could penetrate. I instinctively knew what I learned in the video. And that reinforced my faith.

Now that I have embraced what really happened to me, now that I have embraced how I reacted to those experiences, I feel relieved of the power those experiences had over me. The internal struggle is gone. I feel a lightness, my facial muscles have begun to relax, not just for a few moments, but for days.

The lesson: we must always remember to listen to our bodies. My facial muscles told me that something was not right. It just took me a while to figure out what the problem was ... or actually that it was several things.

Another point to make is that in healing your inner child, you are really healing your adult self. At the start of the process, as I indicated above, we don't usually have much compassion for the inner child. We think it has failed us; we feel it is guilty or are ashamed of it. We do not love our inner child unconditionally, if at all. Or we are in denial about what happened to us as children. All of this negative emotion pushes the inner child away from us, strengthening its feeling of rejection and inadequacy and its ultimate power over us.

But when we go through the process of healing, showing our wounded inner child unconditional love and asking it to speak and tell us how it feels, we are embracing our inner child. And by so doing, we end the struggle between our adult self and our wounded inner child. We, as adults, become healed of the pain and emotions we felt since we were children. The hurt will always remain, but after the healing process our buttons will not be pushed, or at least not as strongly, and we will be able to react to situations that formerly agitated us with dispassion.

But there's more. Having healed your inner child, it is important for you to continue being there for your inner child, like a parent. Remember the inner child is very much alive inside you, just like your smiling toddler.

And so at this stage, it is important to ask your inner child what he wants. And because you have a symbiotic relationship with your inner child, what it wants needs to be experienced by you as well.

When I asked, my inner child said that he wants to experience joy and happiness. And for him to experience joy, I need to experience joy, which is to be free of thought ... emotions, judgments, cravings, attachments, and the eternal "what ifs?"

This message was revelatory for me. I had always said that I want to be free of suffering, free of my ego-mind, and so I need to turn my will and my life over to the care of my true self. My healed inner child was saying that he wants to experience joy and happiness[25] and be free of thought.

These are two sides of the same coin. But as the days passed, I found a big difference in their implementation. What my inner child wants seems easier, more natural. To experience joy and happiness is to experience what's already there, not free myself from something. Perhaps most importantly, there is something very moving to hear your inner child say that it wants to experience joy; it is very motivating; you want to be there for your inner child.

And I am finding that being free of thought in this context is much simpler than turning my will and my life over to the care of my true self. First, it's straight-forward; I don't have to ask how I free myself. Because connecting with my inner joy and happiness changes the direction of my energy flow, as explained in the next section, I am therefore free of thoughts. And if some do arise, I just say "no" to *any* thought or emotion because I know it will interfere with my experiencing joy and happiness at that moment.

Note that being free of thought does not mean that I am not discerning. I am very aware of the situation I am in; I just don't apply the ego-mind's labels to it; instead, I experience it directly with dispassion.

Second, there is no push-back. When I say I want to turn my will over to my true self, my God/Buddha essence, or surrender my ego to it, that is threatening to my ego. When I say I want to experience joy, and freedom from thought is a by-product, I've experienced no push-back.

To put this direction into practice, I start the day off by greeting myself and the world around me with a smile (I look in the mirror and smile) which instantly connects me to my smiling toddler and inner child, to my joy and happiness.

I know I said earlier that when I had practiced Thich Nhat Hanh's "mouth yoga," turning my mouth into a smile,

---

[25] Joy and happiness are not the same thing; both arise internally and are closely related but different. Joy concerns your relation with yourself; happiness relates to your reaction to external things.

the benefit was only momentary. The difference now is that: first, I had in the interim learned of the "heart's embrace" practice which had a profound impact on me, and second, I've connected very deeply with both my smiling toddler and my inner child, and so when I smile, I feel them smiling, expressing themselves, and embracing all aspects of my being and experience. I am at one with them when I smile.

It is also important to set aside time throughout the day to do things for the pure joy of doing them, no other motive, as I described earlier in this book. It also means that when I am doing things that move my life forward, I do them with a smile on my face, without emotion or labels or what ifs.

Many years ago, a monk told me, "Take joy in each moment, in everything you do." I finally understand how, practically, to experience life in that way. It does not mean *finding* joy in the moment or the things I do, because it's already there. No effort is required other than opening myself to it. It just means smiling, touching your positive energy, feeling it flow outward from you as you say "hello" in your mind to everyone and everything, and so being free of thought.

At its core, what I just described is no different than knowing that what's most important to you is peace and happiness and not allowing anything to interfere with that. And yet I am finding this message from my inner child to be even more powerful and easy to implement.

The challenges we face walking the path are many and daily. We are complex people with many parts of our ego-mind and memory impacting how we feel and the actions we take. Becoming aware that my wounded inner child was the avatar of my ego-mind was ground-breaking because it opened up a new path to my healing. Healing my wounded inner child heals my adult self and so will move me further on the path of experiencing peace and happiness and freeing myself from suffering. I am very grateful.

6. Changing the Direction of Your Energy Flow - Creating a Forcefield Around You

All of our lives we have been subjected to an energy flow coming at us, both from the world around us ... our learned experience, what we've been told about ourselves, the negativity and dysfunction in the world ... and from the reaction of our ego-mind to those experiences. We have absorbed countless negative impressions which have overwhelmed our innate inner peace and happiness.

In this chapter I have discussed various techniques to free us from the control of these negative habit-energies. And they work. But as I have frequently noted, the ego-mind will still continue to bombard you with its chatter, seeking to assert itself, requiring you to always be vigilant. This requires great discipline.

There is another technique, however, which builds a virtual forcefield around you which negativity can't breach. It builds on your knowledge that your true self is your heart, and your having opened up the wellspring of loving kindness in your heart.

When you send the compassion and positive energy that is in your heart outward to yourself and others, you change the historic dynamic, you change the direction of the energy flow. And that outward flow of positive energy creates a forcefield.

The most effective way to achieve this positive energy flow is to smile, to see everyone and everything through your heart ... as happened the first time I conjured up my smiling toddler, feeling his hand in mine. I smiled and said "hello" in my mind to everything and every person around me. This goes very much hand-in-hand with the practice of opening up your heart to embrace all aspects of your being and experience.

Smiling to every person includes yourself ... I start every morning by looking at myself in the mirror, smiling, and saying, "Good morning. I love you." It may sound corny, but it works; I feel my heart's unconditional love for myself.

When you smile, you will be a light unto yourself and all others. What does that phrase, "be a light unto yourself," mean actually? I will answer by asking a question: Why does virtually everyone react so positively to a smiling baby? The common statement made is, "Isn't he cute?" or something to that effect. But that doesn't even begin to address what makes us smile when we see a baby or toddler smiling.

When we see a baby smiling, the baby opens up a window for us to a forgotten past. A time when we too experienced unadulterated joy, not brought about by anything in particular, just because our heart was joyful. We smile because the baby is a light unto us. It allows us for a split second to forget all the stuff that we are worried about, that consumes our mind, and just be present and feel the baby's joy reflected in ourselves.

By opening up the wellspring of loving kindness within your heart and letting it flow outward you will open up a window to your heart and be a light unto yourself and to all others. I have experienced that and can attest to its power.

I had done this numerous times, and it indeed put me in a wonderful space. But it only lasted as long as the situation or moment that brought forth this reaction from me.

When my inner child told me he wanted to experience joy and happiness, and I followed through by smiling and saying "hello" in my mind to everyone and everything throughout the day, that activated this positive energy flow as a consistent aspect of my being. It brought about a change in my attitude.

You have a choice. You can go through life, through a day, through a moment and either see all the ugliness and dysfunction that is out there in the world and often indeed within us. Or you can go through life, through each moment and experience joy and happiness, seeing beauty and love, while still being aware of the things that we label ugliness and dysfunction, but without the labels; reacting to them with dispassion, knowing that things are the way they are because it's just the way it is. You will be open to everything that the present moment has to offer.

What you see and experience is a direct product of your attitude. It's similar to the old question, is the glass half full or half empty. If your ego-mind is in control, for some reason it seeks only to see everything that is wrong in the world or in us, everything that in some way it sees as a threat to us. And when we are in that mode, everything that is joy or happiness or beauty is blocked out from our awareness.

On the other hand, if you are present and one with your heart, and you actively seek joy and happiness by sending out your positive energy as well as embrace all aspects of your being and experience, then that is what you will experience every moment. Regardless what the circumstances are, what is going on around you, because of the positive energy you are sending out. This forcefield even blocks out the "background noise" in my life.

You can find joy, happiness, and beauty in nature, which is always present ... the sun, clouds, rain, the stars, regardless the weather. You will find it in yourself because those attributes are present within you, in your heart, your true self. And wherever it is present in the world around you, you will find it. And again, while you will still be aware of things that are not right with the world or yourself, you will not apply pejorative labels to those things and they will not command your focus and block out the joy and beauty that is present.

Regardless how you choose to send out positive energy ... I highly recommend smiling and conjuring up your smiling toddler as the most effective ... you will be nourished, you will nourish yourself, even in the most unlikely of circumstances. For example, I found that since I adopted this practice, riding the NY subway has changed from a blah, somewhat depressing, at times uncomfortable, experience to one of the more spiritual experiences of my day. When I observe my fellow passengers through the eyes of my heart, my smiling toddler, I "see" the beauty and specialness in each person. I see them smiling like the toddler they were and am aware of their true self, their heart. And every once in a while, someone notices the smile on my face, my loving kindness, and sends a big smile back to me. At such moments, I know I have been a light unto that person.

"Why then," the reader may ask, "do we need these other tools, which enable us to say "no" to our ego-mind?" Simply put, we are all human beings. Regardless how disciplined and intent we are, we are easily distracted by the things going on around us.

And so you may create this forcefield, but as soon as you are distracted and stop sending out your positive energy, I can almost guarantee that the ego-mind will take the opportunity to reassert itself. And so you still need the other techniques. You must be as resourceful as your ego-mind.

Sending out positive energy from your heart, being a light unto yourself and others, seeking joy and happiness, beauty and love, is a very powerful practice because not only does it shield you from the negative energy around you and within you, but it creates a state that is close to bliss. You have indeed returned home when you are in that state.

7. Just Do It!

So you now have techniques at your disposal to free yourself from the control of your ego-mind and to put yourself in a space of peace, joy and happiness. But ultimately it comes down to one simple exhortation: Just do it!

By creating a positive energy flow outward from your heart to yourself and the world around you ... by smiling from your heart, saying "hello" in your mind to everyone and everything, and embracing all aspects of your being and experience ... you will create a forcefield that will shield you from the negative energy of your ego-mind and life experiences.

But in those moments when you're distracted, which initially will likely be more often than not, and the forcefield is thus down, you will just have to say "no" to your ego-mind when it arises. If you are beginning to feel frustrated or agitated, that is your red flag. Stop. Be compassionate and gentle but firm with your ego-mind. Your peace and happiness depends on it and nothing is more important.

Saying "no" will be easier because having practiced the heart's embrace, "Not me!" and healing your inner child, you will lessen both the frequency and the intensity of your feelings and perceptions when they do arise. But they will still arise.

To do this it is essential that you be present at all times and have the will to meet your ego-mind head-on and stand your ground when it arises. There can be no equivocating, no bargaining with the ego-mind (we've all been through that fruitless process).

The reward will be peace, joy, and happiness.

8. Bringing It All Together

There is one last step to which "just do it" applies. In this book, I have counseled how you should act to take control of the struggle between your true self and your ego-mind. I have shown how you, as the "observer" of yourself and that struggle, have control over whether you experience peace and happiness or suffering. One can in this way progress very far on the path and experience much inner peace and happiness.

That may be as far as you want or need to go. But I would be negligent not to make you aware of one more step that would bring all of this together and provide an even stronger foundation for your spiritual work.

I've assured you that you will experience much peace, joy, and happiness by undertaking the exercises I've described. I've further noted that how successful your effort is depends on the extent to which you have identified with your true self, your heart, not your ego-mind. At the same time, I've been very frank that your ego-mind will always be there ... these exercises are not about getting rid of the ego mind ... and so you will likely experience at times at least some low level of ego intrusion, possibly the type of "background noise" that I describe.

When meditating one morning I realized that the reason why I still experience ego intrusion, even though to a far lesser extent, is that there is still a lot of "I" in my practice, and therefore in me. "I," as observer, was still in charge. For example, "I will open up the well-spring of love in my heart," "I will open my heart to embrace all aspects of my being and experience." I realized that this constant use of "I" was reinforcing the ego-mind.

On meditating further, the resolution of this came to me in two parts: "Get over yourself" and "It's your true self that will do these things, not the 'I'." And so this section is about more closely identifying with your true self.

Interestingly, I had recently been to a presentation

given by a philosophy professor regarding how to use philosophy to handle mid-life crises. Afterwards, I thought that the real answer was the advice, "Get over yourself."

I mean this not in the sarcastic way the phrase is often used, nor as meaning that people should not be aware of their value or talents. Rather, I mean that after learning that your true self is your heart not your ego-mind, and that all your feelings and perceptions are just a product of your ego-mind and are the cause of your suffering, one comes to the realization that whatever is going on around you, whatever is being done to you or in the past was done to you or may be done to you in the future, has nothing really to do with *you*. It's all about others.

Thus, there is no reason to take things personally. If something nevertheless affects us in a direct practical or emotional way then it deserves a response, but not an ego-driven one. There is no need or reason to "deal" with these things in an emotion-laden manner.[26] Instead, you can go forward doing the things that are important to you, the things that nourish you; you can be who you are while, as always, being aware of the way things are, the situation you are in, and what needs to be done.

There is another aspect to getting over yourself, and that is realizing that in the larger scheme of things your life is like a grain of sand. Your life definitely has meaning in

---

[26] The reader may wonder how this meshes with the counsel I gave earlier in this chapter regarding processing incidents that cause deep anger. The answer is that most of us do still take such things personally and so they need to have a spiritual, emotion-free, resolution. If one is at the stage, however, where you have been able to truly get over yourself, then, while still aware of the hurt caused, there are many situations where you would just walk away from it because you would feel no injustice, no anger. But if the damage was real, practical or emotional, then you would respond in an emotion-free way as suggested. Bottom line, the advice in both sections is consistent. In the first, the need to speak the truth was a way of resolving anger; here the need to speak the truth is purely for its educational value.

that you offer joy to others and you make a difference in the life of others. You do good and are important in that sense. But when viewed against the background of the world, let alone the universe, you acknowledge that you are just a tiny speck. And so you get over yourself by letting go any feelings of self-importance.

Feeling self-important, feeling that everything revolves around you, feeling that you are special is a terrible trap. When you have those feelings, you will always expect to be treated a certain way and when you're not you will suffer.

When, however, you have this awareness and act on it, letting go those feelings, you experience more consistent peace and happiness because you are truly free, doing what *you* want to do; you are being true to yourself. You have no expectations. When you are over yourself you can more easily affirm that you have everything you need inside yourself to be at peace and happy. And that regardless what life throws at you, all will be well because you will continue to do what's important to you and be yourself.

And when you're in this state, you have no reason or need to have any desires because you have everything that's most important to you ... you're doing what you are meant to do and you are being yourself and experiencing peace and happiness. What more could one desire? The ego-mind could obviously come up with lots of things, but that's the point.

Yes, there will still be things that you may want to do to improve your life in various ways, but these do not become desires, they don't become something that your peace depends on. You'll think, "If it happens, great. If if doesn't happen, that's ok too."

You will also realize that your ego-mind adds and has added nothing positive to your life. To confirm this intuitive feeling, I reviewed the events in my past that were important positive moments. And I found that all of those occurred because of the guidance of my heart. My ego-mind was not the catalyst for my doing any of those things. To the extent that my ego-mind involved itself, it instead created problems by creating expectations and goals, rather than just being satisfied by the process, the journey.

When you understand these truths and act on them, getting over yourself, you will in effect be one with your true self. And the last barrier to your fully turning your will and your mind over to your true self disappears. You will have no fear of an ego-free life.

Because you will fully identify with your heart, your true self, you will affirm that it is your true self that will open up your heart to embrace all aspects of your being and experience, observe everything through your heart, open up the well-spring of loving kindness within you, be present and grateful every moment of the day, and allow you to live your life well, which is to be at peace and happiness.

Reflecting that understanding, you will note when you read the suggested affirmations in the next chapter that I say "I/my true self" does such and such. That not just reflects your understanding but puts you in the care of your true self.

When you reach this stage of your practice, although your ego-mind will still be part of you and will no doubt try to make itself felt, it is highly unlikely that you will succumb to its entreaties, to the pull of its emotions, because the ego-mind no longer has power over you. You are free at last. You may still at times experience the background noise of your past, of your ego, but it will not drag you down. You will be aware of it and immediately turn your mouth into a smile, feeling your inner joy and light, embracing everything, dispelling its presence.

Chapter 4:
Staying Grounded - Being Present

In order to change your reaction to things, to exercise your intent to meet your ego-mind head on and stand your ground when it arises, you must be aware, free of emotion, of what is happening at the moment. Because of its importance and difficulty ... we are so easily distracted ... staying grounded, being present, being aware is the focus of this chapter.

Finding inner peace is difficult for two primary reasons. The first has been addressed in the previous chapters. Because of our life experience, we've been trained to think about ourselves and the world around us in ways that are not healthy and cause us suffering. We have lost contact with our true self ... our heart, our God/Buddha essence. The first three chapters of this book have shown you how to rediscover your true self and free yourself from suffering, from the control of your ego-mind, thus finding inner peace.

The second reason, which has been touched on, is that although you may make substantial progress in finding inner peace, the world around you will not stop acting in dysfunctional ways. That is just the way it is. You will continue to experience things on a daily basis, sometimes almost a moment by moment basis, that will push your buttons and your ego-mind will continue reacting with its habit-energy, *if you are not present, aware.*

"What does 'being present' mean?" Bottom line, being present means being free of your ego-mind at that moment. It literally means that you, which is to say your thoughts, are nowhere else but the present. You are not thinking of anything other than what you are doing and where you are in the moment. And you are experiencing the present directly, free of labels, free of emotions, having embraced all aspects of your being and experience, past, present, and future, and so nothing offends. NOTE: This does not mean that you never think about the future; that is after all an essential part of life. But it is important that it be done at a self-designated time, *and* in the right manner ... aware, free of emotion.[27]

This is only possible if you are free of your ego-mind, because your ego-mind is always applying labels and is never in the moment; it is always thinking about something else ... past, future, or even today. "How so today?" you ask. Because an hour from now, even a minute from now, is the future. And it always reacts with emotion.

The clarity you have achieved in rediscovering your true self unfortunately will not magically apply itself to your daily life and end your suffering. It is only by increasing your moments of awareness, your moments of being present, through a disciplined practice (meaning how you approach your whole life) that you will be able to apply what you have learned and find inner peace with consistency.

The challenge we therefore face for the rest of our lives is to stay grounded ... to be present and as aware as possible ... every day, throughout the day. Only then will we be truly free and in control of ourselves.

Then when we encounter dysfunction, rather than our ego-mind reacting to it with anger, fear, frustration, or whatever emotion, we will immediately respond with our heart. And our heart understands that things are the way they are because it's just the way it is.

Then we will see things clearly, aware of the dysfunction but not be agitated. Responding to the moment with dispassion, free of emotion, our minds resting undisturbed, we will release all desire for the present moment to be any

---

[27] See my post, "As a Buddhist, How Do You Think about the Future?" at www.thepracticalbuddhist.com

different than it is, and so be happy and content, free of frustration. Then we will be open to whatever good the present moment offers. Or if our ego-mind does arise, we will be aware of it and quickly say "no" to its guidance and look to our heart.

Only then will be able to exercise good judgment and do what is in our true best interest. Only then will we experience inner peace.

While this may sound like a lot of tedious work, it really isn't. Being disciplined in your spiritual practice and life is difficult and requires great discipline. But the peace and freedom you feel as a result will make the process empowering, enjoyable, and nurturing rather than tedious.

There are five components to staying grounded: meditation, reciting affirmations, reading, becoming part of a spiritual community, and implementing your spirituality in all aspects of your daily life.

1. Meditation

Keeping yourself focused on your path to find inner peace will require great fortitude and clarity of mind. To have such fortitude and clarity in the face of the dysfunction and challenges you will face every day, I highly recommend that you fortify yourself with a daily formal meditation practice. Your spiritual Wheaties, as it were.

I am not going to go into the how-to's of meditation; there are plenty of books and articles regarding that. The essence, however, of all the methods is sitting with proper, erect, posture; concentrating, often on a point on the floor; feeling our breath going in and out; quieting the mind and observing our thoughts, not engaging them; and all the while being aware of our surroundings. Just as important is what meditation is not ... it is not withdrawing; when meditating one never ceases to be part of the flow of life.

Many people find sitting (on a meditation cushion) physically difficult. Either they have back problems, or their knees are sensitive, or their legs fall asleep after a while. None of these problems are unusual and there are ways to sit with good posture that accommodate most physical issues.

If someone, whether a monk or layperson, tells you that the only way to sit is lotus style ... and there are some who teach that ... I would smile kindly and go find another teacher. There are many styles of sitting that are equally effective. You don't even have to sit on a cushion on the floor; you can sit on a chair.

How do you learn how to meditate? Personal instruction is best. So if there is a Buddhist temple or other organization in your area that offers a course in meditation, I would definitely take advantage of it. If you live in a larger city with numerous courses, you might try several different ones as there are various ways of approaching meditation and finding the one that works best for you is worth the effort.

If such a course isn't available, an alternative is to watch a video. You can back this up with readings on meditation.

Once you are clear on how to meditate, then you should set a time for yourself to meditate each day, no matter what is going on in your life or where you may be. I meditate in the morning shortly after getting up. I have found that works well because nothing ever interferes with that schedule. And it works equally well whether I'm at home or traveling.

I cannot overstate the importance of a disciplined, daily meditation practice. Once when I was participating in a discussion group about meditation, people came up with many reasons why they didn't have a daily practice ... things come up, they were tired, they already meditated twice that week, etc. Bottom line, they were not disciplined and because of that their practice was stuck. So although they were serious about their practice in many ways, their ego-mind was still very much in control.

When you start meditating, don't be discouraged if you find it almost impossible to quiet the ego-mind. It will bombard you with thoughts, your "unfinished business," to distract you from your concentration. The important thing is not to engage those thoughts and keep your focus on your breath. One recommendation often made to help keep that focus is to gently say, "thinking," when you catch yourself engaging your thoughts and then return to your breath.

How you come out of your meditation is also important. The idea is to carry over the mindfulness and peacefulness of your meditation and any clarity you found into your daily life to the extent possible.

So when you've finished your meditation, don't jump up and begin whatever is on your agenda. First, sit quietly and continue watching your breath for a few moments with your hands in what is often called "the prayer" position. In Buddhism, it is "the serene heart" position. Then gently stretch your body to wake it up from its sitting position. When you finally get up, be purposeful in looking at your surroundings mindfully and continue in that observing mode as long as you can. Move slowly, do not rush.

Because the goal is to stay grounded throughout the day, it's important that being mindful not be limited to the time you spend sitting on your cushion. This is a spiritual "Duh!" statement, but it needs to be said.

Instead, you should stop at points throughout the day, be aware of your breath, and observe yourself. You may find it helpful to say the phrase, "Breathing in, I'm aware I'm breathing in; breathing out, I'm aware I'm breathing out." Or you may find that chanting or visualizing something peaceful, as suggested in the previous chapter, is more effective for you. The point is to center yourself, bringing your focus back to your heart from whatever distractions or stresses are absorbing you and engaging your ego-mind.

This is especially important when you feel frustrated or angry. Use the awareness of these emotions as a red flag ... your canary in the mine ... that something has carried you away from your heart, your God/Buddha nature and stop, watch your breath, and observe.

If you do not train yourself to be aware and observe yourself throughout the day, then there is no question that you will go through your day under the control of your ego-mind and will not realize you have acted contrary to your spiritual principles until probably the next time you meditate. This may make for powerful teachable moments, but it would be better for your health and sanity to stop yourself at the moment when you are reacting to something and change your habit-energy response.

That said, it is important not to have the expectation of being aware 24/7, or its waking-hour equivalent. You are after all human and that's just not possible. You have not "failed" if your ego-mind takes over at some points during the day. You will always have teachable moments. What you want is to steadily increase the moments during the day that you are aware and that you are in control.

STAYING GROUNDED

In talking about meditation, it is very important to realize what mediation can do and what it cannot. Many people get frustrated because they've been meditating for some time, as well as doing readings and other supportive things, and yet their suffering has not really lessened. They have not found inner peace.

They were looking to meditation to end their suffering, to solve their problems, and it hasn't. But that is not the function of meditation; that is a false expectation.

What meditation does is provide the clarity to see yourself and the world around you free of the effects of your learned experience, free of your ego. It gives you the ability to discern the discrepancy between what your ego is whispering, or more likely shouting, in your ear and what your heart, your God/Buddha nature is telling you.

It then is up to you to take this clarity and apply it to your daily life, to things both large and small, and thus to gradually free yourself from your suffering and ultimately turn your will and your life over to the care of your true self.

2. Reciting Affirmations

Reciting affirmations has two functions. They are very helpful in keeping you focused and thus grounded, not as easily waylaid by your ego-mind. But their main function is their role in helping change the paradigms of your life. I therefore suggest making affirmations part of your daily meditation practice.

How does this work? Over the years, your ego-mind has developed a way of reacting to situations as they arise. These emotions, judgments, cravings, or attachments have become your habit-energies. Your default reaction to what you experience. They have developed into habit-energies because through repetitive use, your brain has laid down pathways, synapses, which connect an input/experience with a particular output/reaction. This is why I often say that people are programmed to react the way they do.

What you are doing by reciting affirmations on a daily basis, and applying/implementing them in your life, is laying down new pathways, new synapses, that will eventually become your new default way of responding, not reacting, to events. I say "eventually" because you should not expect this to happen overnight or even within months. Remember you are changing the habits of a lifetime; it takes time to change old patterns.

Henry David Thoreau identified this process years before science understood how the brain operates. Writing over 150 years ago, he said, "As a single footstep will not make a path on the earth, so a single thought will not make a pathway in the mind. To make a deep physical path, we walk again and again. To make a deep mental path, we must think over and over the kind of thoughts we wish to dominate our lives."[28]

---

[28] H. D. Thoreau, *Thoreau and the Art of Life: Precepts and Principles*, edit R. MacIver, Heron Dance Press, 2006

STAYING GROUNDED

It is important that your affirmations not be recited in rote fashion. Let me rephrase that, they may sound rote, but they must be felt deeply by you. They should express not just what you've been taught, but what you believe. In this way you are making the teachings your own. *If you recite an affirmation that not even part of you believes, it won't work.*

I recite affirmations at the start of my morning practice because they create a mental environment that fosters deeper meditation as well as mindfulness throughout the day. And I do them as part of a walking meditation because by focusing me, my mind tends to be quieted by the time I sit; it is thus a helpful bridge between daily life and sitting meditation. Sometimes the recitation becomes a catalyst, making me aware that there's something I need to meditate on, sit with, which is invaluable.

My walking meditation can take up as much as 10 - 15 minutes before I start my silent sitting meditation. This practice may be unusual, but I have found it very beneficial over the past 25 years.

What follows are some of the things I recite daily, or did for a period of time. If the words are not my own, I have noted the source. (#1-14 are sequential.) Note: As explained in the previous chapter, I have indicated "I/my true self" in the affirmations because it is only through my identity with my true self, my heart, that I am able to do these things. The "I" that is my ego-mind would never do these things.

1. *Breathing in, I'm aware I'm breathing in. Breaking out, I'm aware I'm breathing out.*

2. *I'm aware of the suffering caused by feelings and perceptions and yet know that they are all a product of my mind. And so I/my true self say to them all, "Not me!" And in truth I know that I will be OK, I will be safe[29] regardless what life throws my way because I have returned and will always return home to my true*

---

[29] See appendix for "Safety Defined."

God/Buddha essence, my unwounded heart, and so be at peace and happy. For my heart is light, love, faith, trust, compassion, humility, gratitude, joy, humility, contentment, strength, courage, and wisdom.

3. Breathing in, I'm aware that my life is exactly the way it is right now because it's just the way it is. Breathing out, I/my true self release all desires that my life be in someway different right now and so am happy and content, free of all frustration.

4. Breathing in, I'm aware that all things are impermanent because it's just the way things are. Breathing out, I/my true self release all attachments and so take joy in each passing moment, free of all frustration.

5. I'm aware of the suffering caused by guilt and shame, and yet I know that these emotions are just a product of my mind. They have been thrust upon me by family and society. And so I say to guilt and shame, "Not me!" And in truth I/my true self know that I have no reason to feel guilt or shame because my heart is pure.

To the extent I have done things in the past that harmed either myself or others, and have remorse regarding those actions, that does not make me a bad person. These actions are also the product of my ego-mind. I accept responsibility for these actions, but because they are not a product of my true self, my heart, I do not view myself as guilty or shameful.[30] To avoid harming others or myself in the future, my responsibility and intent is to free myself from the control of my ego-mind.

6. I'm aware of the suffering caused by my craving to have what I do not have or to be someone other than I am, and yet I know that this desire is just a product of my mind. And so I say to it, "Not me!" And in truth I/my true self know that I have everything I need inside myself to experience peace and happiness and I accept

---

[30] For more on "shame," see my post, "Shame" at www.thepractialbuddhist.com

my life as it is right now at this moment. Nothing needs to change for me to be at peace and happy.

7. Aware of the suffering caused by my attachment to emotions, judgments, and cravings, I know they are not me, they are not myself because my true self would not cause me suffering. And so I/my true self say to them, "Not me!" and choose to let them go, to not engage them, and instead go deep within myself to my heart for guidance.

8. I go to my heart, knowing that my true self is my heart; I embrace it and am one with it. And so I return home to my heart and turn my will and my life over to the care of my heart, my true self, my God/Buddha essence now and every moment of every day. And so I see myself and the world around me through the eyes of my unwounded heart and am at peace and happy. My intent is to not allow anything to disturb my heart's peace and happiness.

9. I/my true self open my heart and embrace all aspects of my being and experience - past, present, and future - including my wounded inner child. Thus nothing offends. All internal and external struggle cease to be and my mind rests undisturbed. And so true faith pervades my mind. I know I have everything I need inside myself to be at peace and happy; no circumstance needs to change. And I will allow nothing to disturb my heart's peace and happiness. I am one with my heart.

10. And so at peace, I/my true self am open to receiving all that the present moment has to offer, am grateful, and find happiness in the moment.

11. I/my true self open the well-spring of loving-kindness in my heart and feel it flow out to myself, my inner child, and all others. And so I am a light unto myself, my inner child, and all others.

12. I/my true self know that I have nothing to prove. My only purpose in life is to offer joy to myself and others. And all I need to be happy is to offer joy, to be in the company of loved ones and

friends, to respect my mind, to respect my body, to be in touch with nature, and live within my means.

13. I am aware that my life has meaning in that I offer others joy and make a difference in people's lives. But I know that in the larger context of the world and the cosmos, my life is like a grain of sand. And so I/my true self release all feelings of self-importance. I am over myself.

14. My true self allows me to live my life well, which is to be at peace and happy.

----

15. Breathing in, I breathe in positive thoughts.
Breathing out, I release all negativity.

16. And acceptance is the answer to all my problems today. When I am disturbed, it is because I find some person, place, thing, or situation – some fact of my life – unacceptable to me, and I will find no serenity until I accept that person, place, thing, or situation as being exactly the way it is at this moment.[31]

17. Serenity Prayer, expanded
Grant me: the serenity to understand the things I cannot change, which is the way my life is right now at this moment, and the serenity to just be, to release all desire that my life be different in any way from that way it is right now.

The courage to change the things I can, which is how I relate to myself and to others ... the thoughts I think, the words I speak, and the actions I take.

And the wisdom to know the difference.

18. Wisdom is sitting with myself, going deep within, and knowing that my ego-mind is not my true self. That all emotions, judgments, attachments, and cravings flow from my ego-mind and thus are not

---

[31] SCA, A Program of Recovery, New York, 1990

STAYING GROUNDED

my true self. They weaken me and cause me suffering. And so I do not engage them and return home to my heart.

19. Grant me the courage to free myself from my past, releasing all attachments, emotions, judgments, and desires. And thus have the serenity to experience peace, happiness, hope, self-confidence, and security in the present, lifting oppression and frustration from my heart and mind.

20. Things are the way they are because it's just the way it is.

21. I love myself unconditionally and have compassion for myself.

22. The present is the only reality; all else is thought. Any thoughts I have about the future are just my imagination; the future is unknowable. To ask "what if?" thus creates doubt and anxiety. And so I let go my obsession with "what if?"

3. Reading

There is no shortage of books that seek to guide one on various aspects of the spiritual path. While they all probably have some value, some certainly contain stronger teaching than others.

I will not attempt to put together a suggested bibliography because I am not that well read even in Buddhist literature, let alone the literature of the other mystical traditions or Greek secular philosophy. That's mostly because I've been lucky to have had very wise and strong teachers along the way.

There are a few books, however, that I have read which I've found to be very powerful in their teachings, and so I shall list those for your consideration:

Sogyal Rinpoche, *The Tibetan Book of Living and Dying*
> This was my bible for years. It is beautifully written, accessible, and very relevant for Buddhists who have grown up in Western culture.

Norman Waddell, *The Unborn: The Life and Teachings of Zen Master Bankei*
> While at times this seems like a maddeningly simplistic teaching, its basic truth is very powerful.

J. Krishnamurti, *Freedom from the Known*
> This is not an easy read, but it is profound and powerful in its teaching.

Hazrat Khan, *Personality - The Art of Being and Becoming*
> This is a beautiful Sufi book that taught me much about the heart and the mind. Essential.

P. Rodegast & J. Stanton, *Emmanuel's Book*
> This book is not always easy to digest, but it contains some profound and powerful teaching. I would not be where I am now on the path had I not read it.

If you want to read something about the Buddha's life, I would recommend *The Life of the Buddha* by Bhikkhu Nanamoli. While this is often not an easy read, it is somewhat of a "you are there" experience because the text is taken mostly from the Pali canon. Thus when the Buddha speaks it is as close to his actual words as you can find. When I read this the first time, there were sections that lifted a veil of misinterpretation from aspects of the Buddha's teaching. On further readings I continued to uncover vital teachings. It is a wonderful book.

One final caveat on reading. You should be aware that many books, including ones I have just recommended, contain some teaching that on the surface is misleading or even harmful. What I mean by this is that whether because of translation or the writer not being a native English speaker or just carelessness, a phrase or sentence doesn't convey what the writer meant to convey. So when you read, read with a discerning mind; if something doesn't make sense to you or seem right, stop and examine it as best you can.

FINDING INNER PEACE

4. Becoming Part of a Spiritual Community

You are attempting to change the way you have lived and thought all your life. We need support in this endeavor. But our culture provides us with no support and no role models. And it is not likely that anyone in your immediate circle is walking the path. It is therefore helpful to find a spiritual community in your area and become a part of it on a regular basis.

In doing so keep the following in mind. Whether it be Buddhist, Kabbalah, Sufi, or Gnostic, I suggest a temple or teaching organization because it is very helpful to have a live teacher. Being in the presence of a truly wise person can make a difference. But it's important that you take the measure of the particular teacher, whether he or she speaks to you, because there is certainly a range in the wisdom, teaching styles, and ability of teachers.

The experience, the ambience of the place will also vary from group to group. For example, within Buddhism, you will find quite a range in the temple experience of the different lineages. If you went to a Tibetan temple, a Korean Zen temple, a Japanese Zen temple, and a Nichirin temple, you would find more differences in temple ritual than similarities even though they all share the same teachings of the Buddha.

Even within a particular lineage, you will find differences. For example, when I first went to the Vietnamese Zen temple I attended for 10 years, the two resident nuns included a certain amount of ritual as part of the meditation service and the atmosphere in temple was very quiet and peaceful. When they left, the monk who replaced them placed no value on ritual ... it was all meditation and dharma[32] talk. His teaching method was very confrontational and the atmosphere was at times almost boisterous. Many members of the temple did not like the

---

[32] "Dharma" are the teachings of the Buddha.

monk's style and they stopped attending. Yet his teaching was the most powerful that I have encountered.

The point is that because there is such a variation in teachers and in the practices of the different traditions and religions, if you have various organizations to choose from, I would strongly recommend trying them all to find the one that works best for you. Sometimes it may mean driving or taking public transportation for some distance, but it is worth it to find a good teacher and an atmosphere that resonates with you.

If there is no temple or religious teaching organization in your geographic area, then hopefully there is at least a Buddhist or other religious-based meditation group that sits regularly. Often such groups will listen to or watch tapes of well-known spiritual teachers, or they may do readings from classic texts to stimulate discussion. This can be a very valuable learning experience.

I suggest a religious meditation group, rather than a secular one, because while secular meditation may be very effective at lowering stress, blood pressure, and increasing your calm, it will not provide a path for rediscovering your true self, healing your inner child, and finding inner peace. That said, if a religious-based group is not available, a secular group can still be very helpful to you.

Aside from the support of obtaining teaching, the other important benefit from attending such groups is becoming part of a community. Again, because our culture does not support our efforts to follow the spiritual path and provides no role models ... actually it is antagonistic to our efforts ... meditating with others and experiencing the fellowship of like-minded people provides valuable support to our efforts to live a spiritual life and end our suffering.

5. Applying Spirituality to Daily Life

Each day we make countless decisions that shape our lives ... whether they concern our work, our personal relationships, or other aspects of our life. What voice will we listen to ... our ego-mind or our true self, our heart?

This is an essential part of finding inner peace. Every time we do what our ego-mind wants, we have no peace, we suffer, and our action strengthens its control over us. At the end of the day, if you add up how many times you followed your ego-mind and how many times you followed your heart, that will tell you how much you suffered and how much you were at peace.

We cannot escape the fact that we are part of contemporary culture. Spiritual or not, we live in this world, and it is the way it is. We are part of it ... our work, our family relationships, our various interactions ... all of this happens within the context of and is impacted by our culture. And it is this context that forms our ego, which is the sum of all our learned experience.

But we cannot conform our lives to the teachings of this culture, we cannot act as others act if we seek to experience inner peace and happiness. The two aspirations are diametrically opposed.

This is our conundrum. How do we operate within our culture and yet find inner peace and happiness?

But take heart! It is possible. There is no need to separate yourself from our culture. You don't need to go "off-grid."

The simple answer is to be mindful, aware, and always make decisions from a place of equanimity in a way which does not harm others or yourself. To thine own self be true.

I've given you techniques to use to stay as aware throughout the day as you can. But don't expect perfection ... that's not the name of the game.

As for equanimity, never lose sight of your faith, or perhaps more accurately put developing faith, that regardless what life throws your way, all will be well because you will always return home to your true self, your heart, your God/Buddha essence and be at peace and happy. Remember the truth that you have everything you need inside yourself to be at peace and happy. And never forget all the things you have to be grateful for.

This is especially critical when you put energy and effort into something you want to achieve. Your ego will seek to attach itself to that effort and fill you with cravings and dissatisfaction with the way things are right now. That is your habit-energy.

So when you are engaged in such an activity, remember to go deep within yourself and say, "If it happens, great. If it doesn't happen, that's ok too." That statement will never come from your ego-mind, but it will come naturally from your heart because it does have faith that all will be well regardless.

It's all a matter of maintaining the right perspective and attitude. Maintaining equanimity, remembering what's most important to you, and remembering that things are the way they are because it's just the way it is. And so nothing offends.

As you walk the path to finding inner peace and apply spirituality to your daily life, you will learn to tolerate what you never thought you could tolerate, to endure what you never thought you could endure ... because you realize that these negative feelings are all a product of the mind. Regardless how real they feel, they are not real, because they do not come from your true self, your heart.

Our mind often asks, "What if?" obsessively. And we usually get pulled into that question, creating doubt and fear.

It's up to us to remember that we have no way of knowing what is going to transpire; any thinking about the future is just imagination ... therefore why obsess about what will happen? It's a no-win situation that creates doubt and confusion and so robs you of your peace in the present,

FINDING INNER PEACE

which is where you really need it. Instead, just do the best you can and, again, have faith that all will be well ... although not necessarily in the way you have planned.[33]

Another tool that helps keep things in perspective is to engage in activities that relax you, calm you (beyond the spiritual ones already noted). As adults, most of us have a real deficit in this area. Even activities that we supposedly do to relax us, to get away from things ... like playing golf, playing an instrument, shopping, whatever ... do not relax us because our ego is involved in those activities. They may be a distraction, but they are not calming.

What you need instead is some activity that puts you in touch with your smiling toddler, that innocent being who was and still is free from the burdens of life and most learned experience. Most adults in our culture are closed off to that child; somehow it's not felt appropriate for adults to engage in childlike behavior or activities.

And yet those activities, and the simple laughter that often accompanies them, give one access to the well of innocent joy that only a child experiences. Whether you used to love coloring books, playing simple games, playing with your dog (this is not to be confused with what adults do with their dogs in a dog park), being silly, or whatever, allow yourself the simple joy of immersing yourself in such activities with some regularity. *This is very important.*

These suggestions will help keep you in the mental environment necessary for you to have the strength to apply your spirituality to the decisions you have to make in your daily life. The importance of that to your inner peace cannot be overstated.

I wrote a book, *Making Your Way in Life as a Buddhist*, which presents practical examples of the type of decision-

---

[33] However, planning for the future is a necessary part of life. For lessons on how to do that with equanimity, not obsessively, see my series of four posts titled, "As A Buddhist, How Do You Think About the Future." www.thepracticalbudddhist.com

making we face in our daily lives ... in our personal life, our work, and our lifestyle. And it suggests how they can be traversed in a manner that is consistent with spiritual/Buddhist principles. For the book's Table of Contents, see this book's Appendix I.

In this matter as in all, walking a spiritual path is not easy because there are forces that will seek to pull us in the opposite direction: the siren call of our culture, our ego-mind, and friends and family. I cannot overstate the resistance you will most likely encounter both from within and without. So radical is the shift that is involved for most of us when we choose to apply spiritual principles to all aspects of our lives.

Epilogue
Keep Your Eye on the Prize

A few closing thoughts. Not only must we be disciplined in our practice if we are to progress on the path, but we must have patience and faith.

Changing the paradigms that have been formed over a lifetime and which are inculcated by the prevailing society around us does not happen overnight. It is made more difficult because our ego is our adversary in this effort, and it is strong. Make no mistake, our ego is not our friend ... it does not want the paradigms to change, it does not want us to be free of it.

So as the Civil Rights song said, "Keep your eye on the prize." Do not let the challenges you face deter you. Learn from them and they will make you stronger. Remember that your goal ... to find inner peace ... is well worth what at some times will be a struggle. And this struggle will surely pass ... inner peace is not an impossible dream ... unlike the eternal struggle you would otherwise face leading a life subject to the control of your ego-mind and the influences of our culture.

Appendix I:
Making Your Way in Life as a Buddhist

Table of Contents

Preface: We Are Not Enlightened, Ergo ...	1
1 Building a Platform of Serenity	5
I Believe - The Importance of Faith	7
Aware Breath = Instant Samadhi	10
The Power of Smiling Mindfully	13
Take Joy in Each Moment, in Everything You Do	16
Accepting Ourselves –	
Cultivating a Compassionate Heart	19
Accepting Life	27
Staying Grounded	34
2 How Does a Buddhist Think About the Future?	41
How To Plan Yet Remain Present?	42
How to Desire Yet Not Crave?	44
3 Personal Life	
How to Love	49
Sex	58
Family Relationships	66
Others	75
Death	79
When You're Feeling Down	82
When Really Bad Things Happen	84
4 "Work"	
Choosing Your Purpose in Life	87
Moving Your Career Forward	97
Workplace Relationships	99
5 Lifestyle	101
Meat or No Meat	102
Drinking, Reading, Watching, Listening	105
You As Consumer	109
Your Environmental Impact	111
Charity/Volunteer Work	116
6 Your Buddhist Practice	119

Appendix II:
Safety Defined

The following is a post from my Buddhist blog, www.thepracticalbuddhist.com.

Safety Defined
10/10/2018

We all want to be safe, to feel safe. But what does that mean?

For most people being safe means being safe from external harm. For example, not experiencing physical injury from an accident or devastating illness, not suffering financial harm due to a downturn in the stock market or loss of job, preventing the breakup of a relationship. In general, safety means preventing external events from happening.

People thus spend their lives trying to prevent what cannot be prevented. As the saying goes, "bad things happen." It is an inescapable fact of life. And so people live in fear and are frustrated by their efforts to change their environment to one in which they feel safe. Thus defined, safety or security is an impossible goal.

But for a Buddhist, being safe means something altogether different. It means being free of mental suffering. We understand that we cannot change the way the world is, we cannot change the things that we will experience in life. Things will happen that will cause us harm and pain.

But it is in our power not to experience suffering by any downturns in life, whether it be financial, relational, or health. We cannot escape experiencing the related harm and pain, but we can prevent our suffering because that is a mental state caused by the ego-mind. (See my post, "The Distinction between Pain and Suffering.")

When we are one with our heart, with our true Buddha self, free of the intervention of our ego-mind, when we are free of the emotions, judgments, cravings, attachments, and criticisms that flow from the ego-mind, then regardless what life throws at us, we will be ok, we will be safe, because we have returned home to our heart, to our Buddha mind, and so will be at peace and happy. Even if the darkest things happen to us, we will not lose that state of purity and peace; people may try to defile us, but we cannot be defiled. (See my book, *Making Your Way in Life as a Buddhist.*)

Appendix III:
12 Steps on the Buddhist Path

The following is a post from my Buddhist blog, www.thepracicalbuddhist.com. The 12 steps outlined here are further elucidated in individual posts on the blog. Although this was written in a Buddhist context, its applicability crosses all spiritual lines. If you are not a Buddhist, simply substitute "God essence" or "heart" for references to "Buddha nature."

12 Steps on the Buddhist Path
1/22/2013

In my writing I have noted often that our cravings are really addictions, in that they are things we feel we really need to have in order to be happy; they become compulsions, obsessions. We have no control over our cravings; trying to use our willpower to control them is futile. If we are unsuccessful at satisfying them, we feel terribly frustrated. And if we do satisfy them, not too much time passes before we want more which sets us up for more frustration.

While our craving addictions generally don't cause the kind of harmful effects that alcohol or sex addiction do, nor are they social taboos, they do take a serious toll on our sanity. By causing overwhelming frustration, fear, and anxiety, they impact our opportunity to experience peace and contentment ... they are the core of our suffering. This is not just harmful to us, but without question has a negative impact on all those around us, whether family, friends, or colleagues.

When we think, in our more rational moments, about freeing ourselves from our cravings by accepting ourselves and the world around us as just being the way things are, and having compassion for and loving ourselves unconditionally, we quickly push back against the idea of acceptance because we really don't want to accept. We want our cravings! And our habit-energies usually win out.

We won't accept that our cravings are bad for us. We know that they are, because we know the agony that they put us through, but we nevertheless don't accept that they are unhealthy. Our cravings are normal, we say. Everyone has them. There's nothing socially unacceptable or shameful about our cravings. If they harm us because we can't fulfill them, we feel it's because of something that we're doing wrong; it's our fault. Or we feel victimized. And we certainly don't accept that we have no control over them.

The other morning while meditating, I thought about these issues while reflecting on my experience in a 12-step program. And I had an epiphany. I realized that the reason why, even with good teaching, so many Buddhists find it hard to get beyond a certain feel-good point in their practice, why they are unable to free themselves from their suffering, is their inability or refusal to change their relationship with their addictive cravings ... to accept that they are harmful and that we are powerless over them.

Well, if one is a Buddhist and continues to hold such feelings then one is playing games with oneself. One is trying to have your cake and eat it too. And that just isn't possible.

If I think about the temples I've attended and the dharma talks I've heard, there is very little mention of any of this. Even the very powerful teaching I received that "scratched the itch" ignored this whole issue by going directly to an understanding of the illusory nature of our perceptions and the impermanence of all things. But even with that understanding, even after it was internalized, surrendering the ego to my true Buddha nature was another ballgame. And it all comes back to the power of our cravings and our ego.

As the Buddha said as he set rolling the wheel of the dharma, the origin of suffering is craving. This acknowledgment is the lynchpin of the Four Noble Truths. Without accepting this fact, there can be no real progress on the path.

And so I propose to set forth a new approach to the Buddha dharma ... 12 Steps on the Buddhist Path, an expanded take on the Four Noble Truths and on the Fourfold Path to Freedom which I have presented in my books. (NOTE: Others have used the term, "12 step Buddhism," but in the context of Buddhism as an adjunct to a traditional 12-step addiction recovery program - for example alcohol or sex. What I am proposing is totally independent of any of the traditionally recognized addictions.)

1. Affirmed that what we value most is peace and happiness. Acknowledged that our cravings cause us suffering and make peace impossible. Admitted that we were powerless over our cravings ~ that they were controlling our lives.

2. Came to believe that our true Buddha nature could restore us to peace and end our suffering, and created a platform of serenity through belief in the Buddha dharma, focusing on the good things in our lives, and starting to walk the path of acceptance.

3. Committed ourselves to the path by practicing the Five Precepts and the Six Paramitas

4. Came to believe that all our feelings and perceptions are learned, that they are just a product of our ego-mind. And that our ego-mind is not our true self. Instead we knew that our true self is our heart.

5. Were ready and willing, and made a decision, to surrender our ego and turn our will and our lives over to the care of our true Buddha nature, opening up our heart to embrace all aspects of our being and experience.

6. Came to believe that we have everything we need inside ourselves to be at peace and happy. And formed the intent to not allow anything to disturb our peace and happiness.

7. Came to free ourselves from our cravings and all emotions, judgments, and attachments.

8. Were entirely ready to love ourselves unconditionally and have compassion for ourselves, and to accept ourselves and the world around us as being the way they are because it's just the way it is.

9. Made a list of all persons we had harmed, and became willing to make amends to them all. Made direct amends to such people wherever possible, except when to do so would injure them or others.

10. Continued to be mindful of the arising of cravings, emotions, and judgments. And when they arose, stopped, did not attach to them or engage them, and instead rejected their guidance as not being good for us, and allowed them to subside.

11. Sought through meditation to constantly improve our conscious contact with our true Buddha nature, returning to our self-nature, observing things without the intervention of thought, following the Noble Eightfold Path, and practicing the Six Paramitas.

12. Having had a spiritual awakening as the result of these steps, we tried to carry this message to others who were

APPENDIX III

suffering from their cravings and to practice these principles in all our affairs.

About the Author

After a lifetime of much turmoil, fear, insecurity, and guilt, Ron Hirsch knows something about the search for inner peace. The teaching shared in this book is formed by his own experiences and an understanding of the ego, happiness, and our culture that has developed while walking the path of Zen Buddhism for 25 years, since finding Buddhism at age 49. Hirsch has had a varied career as a teacher, survey researcher, nonprofit executive, composer and writer. His blog, www.ThePracticalBuddhist.com, was selected as one of the top 50 Buddhist blogs on the web. He is the author of three books on Buddhist practice and one ecumenically spiritual work, *Raising a Happy Child*, which was praised as, "A common sense approach to compassion and self-care that all of us need to hear. ... A precious book, well-written and very clear." He is also the author of *We Still Hold These Truths,* acclaimed by James Fallows, National Correspondent, The Atlantic, as "Agree or disagree with his conclusions, the questions he is asking are the right ones for the public this year." He grew up in Reading, Pennsylvania and resides in Massachusetts.

www.ingramcontent.com/pod-product-compliance
Lightning Source LLC
Chambersburg PA
CBHW022106040426
42451CB00007B/151